CONTENTS

ACKNOWLEDGEMENTS

The research project was carried out by the core team led by CB Hillier Parker, comprising Chris Goddard and Stephen Hill, with David Bird and John Duffy from Savell Bird & Axon. They were supported by Dr Brian Raggett, Dr Russell Schiller, Julian Stephenson, Jonathan Langham, and Katy Smith (all from CB Hillier Parker).

The project team would like to express its thanks to all members of the Steering Group for their valuable contribution to the study. The Steering Group comprised officials from the DETR, as well as the following:

RDC:	David Griffin
Boots:	Martin Pope
Stirling University:	Professor Leigh Sparks
RTPI:	Andrew Wright

The project team would also like to extend its gratitude to all the local authorities, retailers, Chamber of Commerce and Trade, and all interest groups who contributed to the study. In particular, the team wishes to thank Sainsbury, Tesco, Safeway, Somerfield and Boots The Chemist for their contribution, and to thank those local authorities which assisted in the case studies.

The project team gratefully acknowledges the assistance of Intermarket Research, Experian Goad Ltd and Verdict Research Ltd during the course of the study.

Cover photograph provided by Jonathan Baldock.

The views and recommendations expressed in this report are those of the research team and not necessarily those of the Department of Environment, Transport and the Regions.

The Impact of Large Foodstores
on Market Towns and
District Centres

CB Hillier Parker

Savell Bird Axon

September 1998

London: The Stationery Office

Department of the Environment, Transport and the Regions
Eland House
Bressenden Place
London SW1E 5DU
Telephone 0171 890 3000
Internet site: http://www.dett.gov.uk/

ISBN 0 11 753478 1

EXECUTIVE SUMMARY

Introduction

1. Market towns have historically been the social and trading focal point for rural England. Their legacy of ancient streets and buildings is a fundamental part of our national heritage. However, as some of their traditional functions are gradually being eroded, there is a genuine concern about their future viability. In particular, there is widespread concern about the effects of large foodstores, particularly in non-central locations, on the economic health of market towns.

2. District centres generally lack the historical associations of market towns, and often have a less clearly defined and established role. However, they also perform an important shopping and community function. A number of the challenges facing market towns, and in particular the growth of large foodstores, are also relevant to district centres.

Purpose of the Study

3. The purpose of this study is to examine the impact of large foodstore development on market towns and district centres. Previous research has failed to address comprehensively the particular concerns facing these centres. This study attempts to address this deficiency.

4. *Vital and Viable Town Centres: Meeting The Challenge*, published in 1994, concluded that only 3% of market towns considered themselves to be vibrant; as many as 15% were in decline. Reasons for this decline include:-

- the pace of industrial and agricultural development;

- increased mobility of shoppers; and

- decline of the economic base that once supported market towns.

5. The House of Commons Environment Select Committee's Fourth Report (1994) highlighted the vulnerability of small town centres to lasting damage from food superstores and other large retail developments. PPG6, published in June 1996, was intended to address some of these concerns, for example by the application of the 'sequential approach' to site selection.

6. Research by Verdict indicates that superstore numbers increased from 457 in 1986 to 1,102 in 1997. Superstores have increased their sales value of total spend in groceries from 29.9% in 1987 to 53.7% in 1996. As food retailers continue to focus on smaller centres, and increase the spread of merchandise, this poses additional threats to the traditional role of market towns and district centres; especially when new stores are located outside town centres.

Research Methodology

7. This study is the most comprehensive assessment of the retail and transportation implications of foodstore development ever undertaken. The study takes an holistic approach comprising:-

- a literature review of earlier research;

- a classification of market towns and district centres;

- a comprehensive survey of all local authorities in England and Wales;

- a survey of all the major foodstore operators; and

- detailed case studies of 9 market towns and district centres.

8. The study has been guided by a steering group comprising representatives of the DETR, Rural Development Commission, the District Planning Officers' Society, retailers and academics.

Previous Research Findings

9.   There has been little published research on this issue to date. The research which has been undertaken has generally been anecdotal, or confined to individual towns, and is inadequate for a number of reasons:-

- there has been no attempt to define or classify market towns and district centres as a particular focus for analysis;

- the lack of before and after assessments means that conclusions as to the effect of large foodstores are rarely based on empirical research;

- there is no 'control scenario' to compare the effects of large foodstore development with the situation had no development taken place;

- there is no common methodology for assessing traffic and transportation effects of large foodstores and comparing findings on a consistent basis; and

- no concerted attempt has been made to effectively integrate retail and traffic impact assessments.

Classification of Market Towns and District Centres

10.   'Market town' is often used as a generic term to encompass a wide diversity of small to medium sized historic centres, and not necessarily those that have a general street/livestock market. Similarly, there is no universal definition of a district centre; their function varies significantly depending on their size and location relative to dense urban areas.

11.   Our analysis has not attempted to identify an all encompassing set of criteria for defining market towns and district centres, but to identify common characteristics. Having explored all the key variables, either singly or combined, our research suggests that the most appropriate and readily comprehensible criterion of the retail role of a centre is the single variable of the multiple retailer count. The number of multiples is a proxy for the size, relative strengths, and the spending power of its catchment. The classification was particularly useful in identifying those centres which are potentially most vulnerable to the effects of large foodstores (see paragraphs 52-55).

Local Authorities' Views

12.   The responsibility for determining planning applications for large foodstore development, and developing policies to safeguard the vitality and viability of market towns and district centres, rests with local authorities. Almost 45% of local authorities consider retail and transport impact methodologies are inadequate, and are concerned about the objectivity of assessments, the lack of reliable base data and the ease with which variables can be manipulated.

13.   We were alarmed at the number of local authorities (20%) which do not require retail impact assessments to be undertaken as a matter of course. A very small minority of local authorities (14%) have attempted post opening surveys. However, these are generally undertaken on an ad hoc basis and are not based on a consistent methodology.

14.   Our research suggests that a combination of the absence of a consistent and workable methodology to assess impact and dearth of available base data has led to significant failings in proper planning control in the past. Many local authorities consider large foodstores have had an adverse impact on the vitality and viability of market towns and district centres.

Retailers' Views

15.   Whilst all major foodstore operators were contacted, the overall response to our survey was mixed. Tesco and Sainsbury provided a wealth of background information both in respect of the questionnaire and additional data for the case

studies. A number of retailers have undertaken their own research into this issue, and both Safeway and Somerfield also provided helpful feedback. We were disappointed that some retailers failed to respond to the questionnaire; there appears to be a stark contrast in the attitude of different retailers towards the planning system and the benefits of undertaking research projects of this type.

16. The significant pressure from foodstore operators to increase their market share means that smaller centres have increasingly become the focus for new store development. Retailers are generally becoming more flexible and specifically are developing store formats targeted at market towns. This is partly a response to the greater restrictions placed on non-central foodstore development in PPG6, and also a recognition on the part of retailers of the benefits of more centrally located foodstores.

17. Food retailers have also expressed concern that new large foodstores can have an impact on other foodstores. One retailer indicated that over 80% of its foodstores in market towns have witnessed impacts of between 3%-40%. One retailer has also indicated that impacts on existing stores are often not confined to one new store opening, but can be impacted upon by a series of new stores over several years. As a consequence, some retailers are taking a more active role in objecting to new out-of-centre foodstores.

18. Our retailer survey revealed that there is a general consensus amongst retailers that a 'good practice guide' is needed to ensure consistency and comparability of impact assessments. Retailers also recognise problems associated with a lack of base data in respect of town centre floorspace, turnover and performance. The provision of this data will serve to reduce the 'guesstimation' of impact assessments.

19. In common with local authorities, retailers do not consider that the planning system provides a satisfactory basis for assessing the scope for, and impact of new large foodstores on market towns and district centres. However, there is some disagreement between retailers and local authorities as to who should provide background information on floorspace data and household interview surveys.

The Impact of Large Foodstores

20. Town centre foodstores tend to underpin the role of smaller market towns and district centres. The effect of competition between retailers within town centres is not normally a material planning consideration. Therefore, the study has focused on the impact of edge-of-centre and out-of-centre foodstores on established centres.

21. Our research identified impacts on market share of between 13%-50% on the principal food retailers in market towns and district centres as a result of large foodstores in edge-of-centre and out-of-centre locations. The decline in market share for the town centre convenience sector as a whole ranged from 21% in St Neots to 64% in Fakenham, and 75% in Warminster.

22. These levels of impact on market share have directly and indirectly led to the closure of some town centre food retailers; increases in vacancy levels; and a general decline in the quality of the environment of the centre. For example, in Fakenham the number of convenience retailers in the town centre declined from 18 to 13; vacancies increased by 33%; and there was a noticeable deterioration of the built environment of the town centre following the opening of an out-of-centre foodstore.

23. Contrary to the widely held perception, our research indicates that impact is not confined solely to other supermarkets. Edge-of-centre and out-of-centre large foodstores sell an increasingly wide range of convenience and comparison goods, and often include other services including Post Office, pharmacy, dry cleaner and cash point.

24. Our research shows that the impact of large out-of-centre and edge-of-centre foodstores is not limited to convenience retailing, but can also adversely affect comparison and service uses. For example, in Fakenham the reduction in turnover of six comparison retailers ranged from 3.7% to 18.9%.

25.   Even in areas with a well developed provision of large out-of-centre and/or edge-of-centre superstores, the addition of a further new superstore can give cause for concern. The long term cumulative impact of a succession of new foodstores can serve to undermine a store or centre over a number of years.

The Practical Consequences of Impact

(a)   Retail Impact

26.   Our research shows that the development of large non-central foodstores can lead to a decline in the turnover of town centre foodstores (38% impact in the case of Tesco in Cirencester). This can and has led to the closure of some town centre food retailers.

27.   There is no available 'benchmark' to determine what percentage decline in turnover will lead to an unacceptable fall in profitability. It will depend on the particular circumstances of individual retailers. A significant fall in turnover can have a disproportionately high impact on the profitability of stores, influencing the ability of retailers to reinvest in store improvements/refurbishment, and ultimately to continue trading. In other circumstances, reduction in turnover has no adverse consequences.

28.   Impact is likely to be most significant for stores which are trading at marginal levels of profitability. Experience shows that foodstore retailers will review store performance, and where stores are performing below a particular turnover/profitability threshold, these stores will be closed. For example, in 1994 Safeway announced the closure of some 17 town centre stores nationwide as part of a company-wide review of stores.

29.   Even where town centre food retailers suffer an impact, but do not subsequently close, there may still be a concern that this will lead to a general decline in activity elsewhere in the centre, and adversely affect the vitality and viability of the centre. This is likely to be most apparent in centres where the centrally located foodstore is the key anchor retailer in the market town or district centre.

30.   Our research shows that market towns and district centres generally have small catchments, which will only support a limited number of large foodstores. Therefore the development of an out-of-centre or edge-of-centre foodstore represents a loss of potential investment in the town centre. New town centre foodstores can act as a catalyst for further investment in town centres.

31.   Where there is no capacity for additional retailing, the opening of an edge-of-centre or out-of-centre superstore is likely to lead to 'disinvestment' in the town centre (i.e. failure to reinvest in store refurbishments, etc). This has implications for the future viability of the individual retailer, and investment in the town centre as a whole.

32.   Our research shows that even the potential threat of an out-of-centre foodstore can adversely affect retailer confidence. In one of our case study towns, there was evidence to suggest this was a prominent factor in some retailers' decision to continue trading in the town.

(b)   Employment – Do Large Foodstores Generate Additional Jobs?

33.   The lack of accurate, comprehensive and disaggregated data at a local level has precluded a thorough assessment of this issue. Any assessment will need to take account of not only changes in the retailing sector, but also the effect on related businesses, e.g. local accountants and tax advisors.

34.   What little research there has been on this particular issue tends to concentrate on the national perspective, and the 'global' changes in employment in retailing. Recent research published by the National Retail Planning Forum concludes that there is strong evidence that new food superstores have, on average, a negative net effect on retail employment.

35.   At the local level, large foodstores are undoubtedly significant employers, although some existing jobs are likely to be lost. We have been unable to find any conclusive evidence of any significant positive or negative impact on the wider local economy as a consequence of new store openings in the case study examples.

(c)   Transport Effects

36.   Out-of-centre stores attract a significantly higher proportion of car borne trade than those in town centres. When people have a car available, they will almost certainly use it to undertake food shopping. This suggests that the mode choice influences the decision where to shop rather than vice versa.

37.   The introduction of a new out-of-centre store tends to lead to a small shift in mode towards the car at the expense of walking, and to a lesser extent, travelling by bus. However, percentage changes are relatively small, which suggests that the majority of people shopping at the new store were already undertaking food shopping by car.

38.   Our case study results show that between 25% and 65% of people visit an out-of-centre foodstore and town centre during the same trip. For out-of-centre stores, this linkage is normally undertaken by car. For edge-of-centre stores, there was evidence at Warminster of a significant level of walking between the two locations. The degree of linkage by walk mode will be strongly influenced by the overall quality and convenience of the route as well as the distance.

39.   Four factors are likely to affect how vehicle travel distance may be altered by a new store. These are:-

- the difference in distance travelled to the new store compared with the old;

- the change in mode;

- the change in frequency; and

- the change in propensity to undertake linked trips.

40.   The change in distance travelled will depend on individual circumstances, but in certain cases, the distance travelled will decrease as people are 'clawed back' from a more distant store to a more local one. This will depend on a range of factors including the current availability of modern foodstores within the local area.

41.   Car use is likely to increase by a small degree as a result of a new store. Frequency of trip is unlikely to be a significant factor. Similarly, there

is no evidence that the propensity to link trips will either increase or decrease.

42.   Available evidence suggests that the change in overall travel distance due to a new store will vary from town to town. In any event, changes are likely to be relatively small in the context of the overall distance travelled for food shopping. It is unlikely that the changes in travel distance will be a determining factor when deciding where to locate a new store.

The Clawback Argument

43.   Significant claims are made concerning the ability of new superstores to claw back trade to the centre in question, and the retail benefits derived from this. Our analysis suggests that the extent to which new foodstores will claw back trade will depend upon:-

- the size and accessibility of the store;

- the location of the store (out-of-centre or edge-of-centre);

- the nature of the catchment area (the range and proximity of competing foodstores); and

- whether any other non-central foodstores have been developed in close proximity to the town.

44.   In our two edge-of-centre case studies, the principal effect of the new stores was to divert trade from the town centre to the edge-of-centre locations, although this result may reflect the particular circumstances of these towns. Where there is already a well established non central superstore (e.g. Tesco in Cirencester) it is unlikely that an additional edge-of-centre store will achieve the same level of clawback.

45.   Our research shows that large, highly accessible superstores are likely to achieve higher levels of clawback than smaller, less accessible stores, irrespective of location. For example, in Fakenham some 46% of the trade of the out-of-centre Safeway is derived from clawback of expenditure. However, in this and other case study towns, this has led to no tangible benefit to the town/district centre.

Linked Trips

46.   The propensity to undertake linked trips depends on four interrelated factors:-

- the extent to which the store complements the town centre/district centre;

- the distance and physical linkages between the two;

- the relative size of the centre as compared with the store; and

- accessibility, parking and orientation of the store.

47.   Shoppers using town centre foodstores are more likely to undertake linked trips in the centre than shoppers using an edge-of-centre foodstore. Similarly, shoppers using edge-of-centre foodstores are in general more likely to undertake linked trips with the centre than those using out-of-centre foodstores. This appears to support the policy preference for town centre or edge-of-centre stores.

48.   The introduction of a new out-of-centre store does not appear to have a significant effect on the propensity of people to link visits to the foodstore and the town centre during the same trip. Some of our case studies show that linked trips have increased following the opening of the new non-central foodstore (e.g. 52% to 63% in Leominster). However, there is no evidence of any significant increase in the use of centres for non-food shopping as a result.

Issues Raised by Edge-of-Centre Stores

49.   Our research shows that distance from and the physical integration of edge-of-centre stores with the town centre both affect the propensity to undertake linked trips. In the case of Cirencester, the edge-of-centre Waitrose is too far from the main centre, and the physical linkages between the store and centre are too weak to generate significant linked trips. Those linked trips which do take place tend to be by car.

50.   In both our edge-of-centre case studies, there was a significant displacement of retailing activity from the town centres; principally as a result of the closure of the town's main town centre foodstores. Whilst neither centre was significantly adversely affected as a whole, neither benefitted from the development of the edge-of-centre foodstores. If the catchment of both these towns had been sufficiently large to enable both the town centre and edge-of-centre stores to continue to trade well, we anticipate that our conclusions would have been different.

51.   We consider that a more thorough assessment of the linkages between edge-of-centre stores and town centres/district centres is necessary, having regard to the factors we have identified. We also consider more comprehensive analysis of the likely impact of edge-of-centre stores on existing centres is required.

Are Small Market Towns and District Centres More Vulnerable Than Larger Ones?

52.   The increasing concentration of retail activity into a smaller number of larger centres means that market towns and district centres will continue to face increased competitive pressures, irrespective of the impact of new foodstores. As the vitality and viability of these centres increasingly relies on their convenience and service function, all market towns and district centres are likely to become potentially more vulnerable to the impact of large out-of-centre and edge-of-centre foodstores.

53.   We consider the extent of a centre's vulnerability will depend on:-

- whether it has already experienced retail impact (a single impact or a series of impacts – cumulative impact);

- the diversity of its role – the strengths of its convenience, comparison and services function;

- the extent to which the centre performs a tourist function;

- accessibility, prominence and general attractiveness of the centre; and

- the size of the centre in relation to any new foodstore proposal.

54. Smaller centres which are dependent principally on their convenience shopping function are generally less able to adjust to a transfer of food trade to less central locations. Where foodstore proposals are disproportionately large compared with the size of the centre, the new store can supplant the role of the centre. Smaller centres therefore require additional 'protection'. (see Policy Implications)

55. Notwithstanding the longer term challenges of retail polarisation, larger centres have a well developed comparison and services function, and tend to be less susceptible to harm from large foodstores. Centres with a clearly defined tourist role, which do not rely solely on expenditure from the local catchment, are also generally more robust.

Towards a Common Methodology (The 'CREATE' Approach)

56. There is a clear need for a common approach to assessing impact. We have identified the critical stages of any retail and traffic impact assessment and have referred to this as a Combined, Retail, Economic And Transport Evaluation (CREATE). This is not a model, but a logical series of steps, which are designed to address all relevant criteria using a comprehensive and consistent range of data.

57. The principal advantages of this approach are:-

- a clear step by step approach;

- the integration of retail and transportation retail impact assessments (in accordance with PPG6 and PPG13);

- survey based (reducing the need for unsubstantiated assumptions);

- a consistent framework for predicting the likely impact of edge-of-centre/out-of-centre foodstores; and

- sensitivity analysis of the principal variables to highlight the effects of different judgements about the likely trading pattern of a new store.

58. By reducing the number of potential areas of disagreement, a consistent and workable approach to assessing impact is less likely to distract from the key areas of concern at public inquiries, and should help minimise the risk of past mistakes occurring in the future.

Policy Implications

59. This study raises significant issues for planning policy guidance for market towns and district centres. Because of their potential vulnerability, guidance should place greater onus on local authorities and developers to adopt a positive approach to sustaining and enhancing market towns and district centres. They should assess thoroughly all potential town centre opportunities before advocating less central proposals.

60. The 'need' for a new foodstore in market towns/district centres should be more clearly defined in PPG6. Where there is no need for a foodstore (i.e. no qualitative or quantitative deficiency), then no additional foodstores should be developed.

61. The current distance guideline of 200-300 m for edge-of-centre locations in PPG6 may be too wide for some small market towns. In addition to the need for strong physical links with the town centre, edge-of-centre development should be of an appropriate scale relative to the centre, and complement the existing retail offer. Local

authorities need to help 'create' linkages to ensure edge-of-centre stores complement rather than supplant the convenience shopping role of these centres.

62.   All foodstore proposals over 1,000 m^2 net sales, on the edge of, or outside market towns and district centres, should be accompanied by a Combined, Retail, Economic And Traffic Evaluation (CREATE). It is unlikely to be necessary to carry out such assessments for fully integrated town centre developments, as these will be likely to contribute to the vitality and viability of the town/district centres.

63.   PPG6 should recognise more explicitly that vitality and viability assessments should be undertaken on a regular and consistent basis; the pattern of change over time is crucial. The most relevant vitality and viability indicators for small market towns and district centres are retailer representation and retailer performance, vacancy levels, and the state of the town centre environment.

64.   Market towns and district centres are particularly vulnerable to the cumulative impact of a succession of stores over a number of years. The impact of large foodstores may not become evident for several years (e.g. vacancy levels). Impact assessments should quantify the cumulative impact of a succession of developments. When there is already a well developed provision of out-of-centre foodstores, a cautious approach to any further non-central development may be warranted.

65.   Given the challenges facing market towns and district centres, it is critical that local authorities develop proactive strategies for these centres. Town centre management has become increasingly prevalent in many towns. It may not be appropriate for each centre to have a dedicated Town Centre Management Initiative – a single Town Centre Manager responsible for a number of smaller centres can be an effective compromise.

Additional Data Requirements

66.   During the course of the research for this study, we have identified a number of deficiencies in the availability of base data. These include:-

- An objective means of measuring town centre turnover/performance;

- Reliable floorspace data for all town centres and district centres;

- The need for additional research into cumulative retail impact; and

- The need to provide a workable methodology for assessing town and district centre boundaries.

Conclusion

67.   Our research has shown that large foodstores can and have had an adverse impact on market towns and district centres. The level, and consequences, of impact will vary depending on the particular local circumstances of the centres concerned. Smaller centres which are dependent to a large extent on convenience retailing to underpin their function, are most vulnerable to the effects of larger foodstore development in edge-of-centre and out-of-centre locations.

68.   It is vital that those responsible for the future of market towns and district centres take positive steps to improve the range and quality of food shopping in these centres, and adopt a cautious approach to considering the location and likely long term consequences of the development of large foodstores in non-central locations.

CHAPTER 1
Introduction

Context

1.1   In November 1995, the then Department of the Environment (now the Department of the Environment, Transport and the Regions) commissioned Hillier Parker and Savell Bird Axon to undertake a wide ranging research study to assess the impact of large foodstores on market towns and district centres. The original timescale for the research has, in agreement with the DETR, been extended to enable a comprehensive and systematic analysis of the key elements of the study.

1.2   The challenges facing market towns and district centres are complex. For many, their traditional role has been undermined by the pace of industrial and agricultural development, and more recently by the increased mobility of shoppers. For some, this has manifested itself in the decline or closure of traditional markets, and associated services and jobs. As a consequence, the more mobile sectors of rural communities are not as dependent on market towns as they once were.

1.3   An additional pressure on smaller centres has come from the significant growth in new retail formats, and in particular, the development of large foodstores, which threaten to undermine the traditional role of market towns. The shift in focus of the main foodstore operators towards smaller centres is partly an economic imperative, namely to fill gaps in their store representation, but also a reflection of the increasingly limited development opportunities in larger centres.

1.4   The development of foodstore formats below the conventional threshold for superstores of 2,500 m² sales floorspace can still have significant consequences for small centres. By virtue of their historic street patterns and conservation area status, many market towns cannot physically accommodate large foodstores in their town centres. Our research has therefore not been confined to superstores, but has considered the implications of all large foodstores which may affect market towns and district centres.

1.5   Whilst concern about retail impact generally on town centres has been recognised for some years, the particular issues facing market towns, and their potentially greater susceptibility to adverse impact, has been recognised only relatively recently. In 1994, *Vital and Viable Town Centres: Meeting The Challenge* highlighted the changing role of market towns, and identified the aggressive competition between grocery chains to secure sites as a contributory reason for the decline in some towns. Additional research by the Rural Development Commission has also identified the increase in out-of-town shopping centres as a significant problem facing small market towns.

1.6   These concerns are recognised by the House of Commons Environment Select Committee in its Fourth Report; the Government's response to the Report; the subsequent Consultation Paper on PPG6; and in the latest revision to PPG6 (June 1996). In its Report of March 1997, the Environment Select Committee reaffirmed its concern about the issues affecting market towns, and in particular, the potentially adverse effects of large foodstores. In its response, published in July 1997, the Government recognised the need for impact assessments, and anticipated that the research commissioned in this study should help to provide guidance on the most appropriate approach to impact assessments, and how to interpret the impact of large foodstores on such centres.

1.7   Prior to this study, much of the evidence to support the contention that market towns have been adversely affected by large foodstores was anecdotal and based on intuitive reasoning. This report attempts to address this deficiency, and through a comprehensive range of surveys and case studies, add significantly to the collective understanding of the subject. This study puts into context the practical consequences of large foodstore openings in market towns and district centres, and is intended to provide retailers, developers and local authorities with guidance to assist them in responding to the need for new foodstores.

Approach to the Study

1.8   In order to provide as comprehensive an assessment as possible, we have employed an holistic approach combining a mix of desk-top research and original surveys. The study has been undertaken in three self-contained stages, each of which builds on the results of the previous one. This agreed approach has extended the original timescale of the research, but in our view provides added weight to our conclusions.

1.9   Stage One includes a literature review, which considers the features that define market towns and district centres, and highlights the principal issues facing them. The review examines previous research into the effects of large foodstores on market towns and district centres, and examines the criteria which may be used to identify different sizes and types of market towns.

1.10   Stage One includes a detailed local authority survey to identify those market towns and district centres which have experienced foodstore development since 1990. We have also undertaken a survey of the principal foodstore operators to determine their views as to the most

appropriate means of measuring the impact of new foodstores, and their experience of the impact of superstores on their town centres.

1.11   An integral part of the research has been the individual case studies, which have collectively provided a comprehensive reflection of what has happened in practice in a variety of different market towns and district centres. In order to establish a robust approach, which is sufficiently sensitive to identify and measure both the positive as well as negative effects of large foodstores, a pilot survey of Cirencester was undertaken as part of Stage One.

1.12   This approach was fine-tuned and employed subsequently in Stage Two of the research, which comprised eight additional case studies. These were undertaken in two tranches to cover as comprehensive a mix of market town and district centre scenarios as possible. Each case study comprised two elements; first, an assessment of changes in a pre-selected range of criteria, based on a post-opening household interview survey; and second, an assessment of the centre's vitality and viability and how it had changed.

1.13   The third stage of the research draws on the results of the detailed case studies to test the general conclusions of the retailer and local authority surveys. This assesses whether many of the claims made both in favour of and against large foodstores, and their potential impact on market towns and district centres, are justified. In particular, we assess whether there is any substantive evidence to suggest cause and effect between the development of out-of-centre foodstores and adverse effects on established centres. In addition, we draw out the general lessons which can be applied from our analysis when considering new proposals in different types or sizes of market town and district centre.

CHAPTER 2
Literature Review

2.1   We have divided our literature review into a number of self-contained themes, which seek to identify the key issues facing both market towns and district centres.

Definition of Market Towns and District Centres

(a)   Market Towns

2.2   There is no universally accepted definition of what constitutes a market town. According to the Concise Oxford Dictionary, a market is "the gathering of people for the purchase and sale of provisions, livestock, etc..., especially with a number of different vendors". Not surprisingly, the dictionary goes on to define a market town as "a town where a market is held".

2.3   In particular, "Market Town" is often used as a generic term to encompass any small town with some of the features traditionally associated with market towns, i.e. relatively small towns in rural areas, which rely to a large extent on food shopping.

2.4   In an attempt to clarify what constitutes a market town, the DoE publication, *Vital and Viable Town Centres: Meeting the Challenge*, identified a number of key characteristics of market towns:-

"Market towns have long been places to trade, and though in many cases the old agricultural markets are closed, most still retain regular outdoor general markets, with a strong emphasis on food".
(DoE, 1994).

2.5   The study recognises that a number of market towns have, for the most part, retained their historical street pattern, and that many

Saffron Walden town centre, Essex.

buildings were constructed on traditional long, narrow plots with limited street presence. Many of these are now listed, and/or are within designated Conservation Areas.

2.6   More recently, the Rural Development Commission sponsored a conference entitled *Putting the Heart back into Market Towns*. This was specifically aimed at those interested in promoting the vitality and viability of smaller towns. A series of features of market towns were identified:-

- Historic places of trade, with a legacy of ancient streets and buildings;

- Generally anchored on food and convenience retailing;

- With small populations of 3,000-25,000 and rural catchment areas;

- Still a meeting place for young and old;

- Somewhere interesting to visit, given increased leisure time; and

- Providing a narrowing range of services e.g. buses, banks, bars.

2.7   Research undertaken by the Rural Development Commission identified a total of 887 small towns in England with populations between 3,000 and 15,000. Within these towns, there are 209 general retail markets and 59 livestock markets. The following conclusions were drawn:-

- Most counties with general retail markets are sparsely populated and primarily agricultural in character. They are mainly within East Anglia and the rural north;

- Counties with livestock markets tend to be located in the north and the west of the country;

- Of the 210 small towns with general retail markets, only eight operate on a daily basis. 140 have weekly markets and 61 have markets that operate on a more frequent basis, with a typical frequency of two to four times a week; and

- Of the 59 small towns with livestock markets, 36 have markets that operate on a more frequent basis. (RDC, 1996).

Woodbridge town centre, Suffolk.

Porchester district centre, Hampshire.

2.8   Shopping studies undertaken by Hillier Parker in Southwell, Beverley and centres in East Hampshire have confirmed the importance of food shopping in smaller towns. In general, town centre foodstores perform a 'top-up' food function rather than catering for bulk food purchases. Nonetheless, in the context of their relatively restricted catchment areas, these stores are very important to the continued vitality and viability of these centres.

2.9   Similarly, a region-wide study of shopping in Dumfries and Galloway undertaken by Hillier Parker in 1996, highlighted the significance of food shopping in smaller market towns; some of which are located in remote rural areas. In contrast to small towns which are relatively close to higher order centres with large superstores, a number of food stores in more remote market towns perform a main food as well as a 'top-up' food function. A similar conclusion, albeit in different types of market town, was reached in a Shopping Study undertaken of the six centres in Suffolk Coastal district area by Hillier Parker in 1997.

2.10   Internal research undertaken by Sainsbury of a broad sample of country towns has revealed some distinguishing characteristics of country town shoppers:-

- *"The percentage of ABC1 categories is significantly lower than the national average, with C2 DE tending to form a higher proportion of the country town population;*

- *The population within country towns is generally older and the percentage of pensioners is higher than the national average. Country towns are often attractive places to live for older people in retirement;*

- *Car ownership is more widespread in the catchment areas of country towns than the national average;*

- *Country town shoppers tend to be quite promiscuous in their choice of store in an attempt to find a wider range of goods and to make the experience more interesting".* (Williams, 1995).

2.11   For the purpose of our detailed analysis of market towns, we have concentrated on small towns serving a rural hinterland with a population of between 5,000-30,000. This reflects the concern generally about the vitality and viability of smaller town centres, and in particular the extent to which these towns may or may not be affected by large food stores.

(b)   District Centres

2.12   There is no widely acknowledged definition of a district centre. District centres, by their nature, tend to be less homogenous than market towns. Depending on their size and location relative to dense networks of urban areas, the function of district centres can vary considerably.

2.13   For example, as has been highlighted by Sainsbury in its response to our retailer survey, a free-standing supermarket with a modest number of unit shops or in-store concessions may perform the role of a district centre, within a local residential area, but may not warrant the 'protection' as a centre in the terms of PPG6. This is a policy issue which requires clarification.

2.14   Sainsbury has also indicated that there can also be a number of questions regarding the relationship of a single large supermarket with an existing local shopping centre. This is particularly a problem in suburban centres in metropolitan areas, and especially in London. These sentiments are similar to those expressed by other food retailers. It is becoming increasingly difficult to define "traditional" district centres in metropolitan areas where the role of local and district centres has evolved over time.

2.15   In terms of identifying principal characteristics, Annex A of PPG6 (June 1996) defines district centres as:-

"Groups of shops, separate from the town centre, usually containing at least one food supermarket or superstore, and non-retail services such as banks, building societies and restaurants."

This contrasts to what PPG6 defines as a 'Local Centre':-

"…small grouping usually comprising a newsagent, a general grocery store, a sub-post office and occasionally a pharmacy, a hairdresser and other small shops of a local nature."

2.16   In common with market towns, district centres rely on a strong convenience retail offer to underpin their economic health, and to enable them to service the everyday retail needs of their local catchment areas.

The Challenges Facing Market Towns

(a)   The Changing Role of Market Towns

2.17   *Vital and Viable Town Centres: Meeting the Challenge* highlighted the changing role of market towns, and suggested that whilst many had not been overwhelmed by industrial development, the pace of change in recent years has presented greater challenges. Agricultural developments and increased shopper mobility have, to some extent, undermined the traditional role of market towns. Shoppers increased expectations, in terms of the variety and range of shopping facilities on offer, means that market towns are often less able to compete with larger centres. As a consequence, more mobile sectors of rural communities are less dependent on market towns; to less mobile sectors, they may retain a critical role.

2.18   Other common problems facing market towns include the decline in small family run businesses, and the trend amongst multiples to operate fewer, larger branches. This leads to a fall in retailing diversity, and as a consequence, encourages locals and potential visitors to shop elsewhere, particularly in larger centres. This polarisation of retailing continues to underline the dominance of higher order centres, often at the expense of smaller market towns and district centres.

(b)   Convenience Retailing in Market Towns

2.19   A further challenge to market towns, and town centres in general, has been the increase in out-of-town supermarkets and shopping centres. The potential threat of these new retailing locations was identified in 1990 in the government publication *This Common Inheritance*. This accepted that out-of-town shopping centres had advantages, creating new jobs, choice and providing easier access to a wide range of goods, but sounded a note of caution:-

"The Government's guidance to planning authorities already emphasises the need to ensure that their planning decisions do not damage the vitality and viability of town centres as a whole". (HMSO, 1990).

2.20   Since the publication of *This Common Inheritance*, concern over the impact on towns, and in particular smaller towns has increased significantly. *Vital and Viable Centres* examined 338 towns and cities in England & Wales. It concluded that market towns were making less progress than large cities, suburban centres, industrial towns or historic towns and resorts – even though the populations are rising. Of the 131 market towns surveyed in the report, only 3% indicated that their own town was vibrant. As many as 15% said their own town centre was in decline.

2.21   The Report identified that part of the problem of decline stems from the dependency of most market towns on convenience shopping:-

"They have, therefore, been particularly vulnerable to the aggressive competition between grocery chains to secure sites. They have often been facilitated by the availability of sites off by-passes, and relaxed planning regimes. Smaller towns often lack the resources to match the sophisticated developer". (DOE, 1994).

2.22   During the 1980's, the main national food retailers concentrated their store opening programmes on major towns and cities, but since the early 1990's have increasingly turned their attention to smaller towns. This is reflected in Sainsbury's store development policy:-

"With our existing store portfolio we are currently piloting our Central Store Concept in three town centre locations... However, we intend to supplement this activity with further new store development. We may not be developing as many large superstores as in the past, but we will continue to explore new formats, perhaps the most exciting of these is for smaller 'Country towns'". (Williams, 1995).

2.23   This increasingly flexible approach to new store development is evidenced in Sainsbury's June 1997 Store Format Guide:-

"The size of a new build Sainsbury's supermarket can range now from 8,000 ft² up to 50,000 ft² (sales) depending on location and obviously planning consent".

More specifically, in the context of its smaller stores, Sainsbury has identified the following formats:-

- City Centre/High street stores (8,000-10,000 ft² sales area);

Table 1 Sales Value of Grocers: Out-of-Town vs High Street 1987-1996			
Year to December	Total Grocers Retailers £m	Grocery Superstores £m	Superstores as % of all grocery outlets
1987	30,690	9,188	29.9
1988	33,921	11,147	32.9
1989	36,748	14,285	38.9
1990	40,382	17,447	43.2
1991	44,420	20,266	45.6
1992	48,458	22,750	46.9
1993	51,689	25,520	49.4
1994	54,920	28,595	52.1
1995	59,362	31,465	53.0
1996	63,400	34,055	53.7
Source: Verdict Analysis (1997)			

Table 2 Grocers Shops By Type, 1961, 1980 and 1997

	1961		1980		1997	
	Number	%	Number	%	Number	%
Multiples	17,000	11.6	6,700	11.5	5,500	19.1
Co-ops	14,000	9.5	6,370	11.0	2,300	8.0
Independents	116,000	78.9	45,000	77.5	20,900	72.9
Total	147,000	100.0	58,070	100.0	28,700	100.0

Source:IGD/Verdict (1998)

- Infill stores (10,000-20,000 ft^2 sales area);

- Small town stores (12,000-20,000 ft^2 sales area).

2.24   Research undertaken by Verdict shows that the proportion of total grocery trade attracted by superstores has increased from 29.9% in 1987 to 53.7% in 1996 (Table 1). Of course, this trend is itself partly attributable to the development of new superstores over this period. This also reflects the increasing propensity of superstores to incorporate a wider range and diversity of products (i.e. fresh meat and fish counters), largely at the expense of smaller and more specialist food retailers.

2.25   Concurrent with the fall in market share of more specialist grocers and the growth of multiples, there has been a more general decline in the number of outlets. Research published by Verdict in January 1998 indicates a significant reduction in the total number of grocery retailers of all types since 1961 (see Table 2). In terms of absolute numbers, the independents have witnessed the most closures, although there has also been substantial rationalisation amongst the multiples and Co-ops of their older smaller stores. This is consistent with analysis undertaken by Goad, which shows that the number of convenience retailers as a proposition of total town centre units (as defined by the Goad Plan) fell from 12.0% in 1990 to approximately 9% in 1997.

Table 3 Floorspace of Grocers – Out-of Town vs High Street

Year to December	Total grocers retailers floorspace million ft^2	Grocery superstores million ft^2	Superstores as % of all grocers outlets
1987	73.0	17.5	24.0
1988	74.1	19.2	25.9
1989	77.2	22.1	28.6
1990	80.9	25.2	31.1
1991	84.7	27.4	32.4
1992	88.1	29.4	33.4
1993	91.0	32.1	35.3
1994	94.2	35.7	37.9
1995	96.4	37.3	38.7
1996	98.1	38.6	39.2

Source: Verdict Analysis (1997)

Henley town centre.

2.26   Although store numbers have fallen, Verdict research suggests that the average size has increased significantly to accommodate a broader range of products. Modern grocery superstores often include a wide range of non-food products such as clothing, health and beauty, housewares, and home entertainment. They also offer services such as a pharmacy, post office and cash point banking facilities. Improvements to supply chains have reduced the area needed for storage, and this has been replaced by more sales space with a wider range of goods.

2.27   As many market towns have historical street patterns, often within conservation areas, opportunities to develop large town centre food stores can be limited. The pressure for development of new food stores outside these towns or on the edge of them is therefore increasing. *Vital and Viable Centres* suggests that:-

"Half of the market towns who answered the question on the effects of an out-of-town food superstore said that it had a possible negative or major adverse impact, compared with 13% who thought it had been beneficial". (DOE, 1994).

2.28   Conversely, food store operators claim that aside from the commercial considerations, the provision of out-of-centre/edge-of-centre food stores have benefits in reducing the need for and length of existing car journeys. At a Public Inquiry in 1994 into an out-of-centre superstore at Stroud, the Inspector referred to the provisions of the then current PPG6 which identified the distinctive roles and benefits of superstores and smaller shops, concluding that the two-tier hierarchy in food shopping, as advanced by the applicant (Sainsbury) i.e. bulk food takes place in superstores and top-up shopping in smaller shops, is well established. It was suggested that specialist trades and supermarkets are 'little affected by supermarket developments', because 'bulk shopping trips will already have transferred to existing superstores'.

(c)   Recognition of the Potential Threat to Market Towns

2.29   The need to ensure that out-of-town shopping facilities do not damage the vitality and viability of town centres has been recognised since 1986. However, it was not until the House of Commons Environment Select Committee's Fourth Report (1994) that the particular concern of smaller towns was formally recognised and highlighted.

2.30   The Environment Select Committee argued that developers should have to demonstrate that their proposals would not harm town centres. The onus should be placed on developers to show that no harm would be caused to the vitality and viability of town centres. Although this suggestion was aimed at all town centres, specific consideration of smaller towns was urged:-

"Given the vulnerability of small town centres to lasting damage, we recommend that a proper study be urgently undertaken to assess the effects of out-of-town developments on town centres. In the meantime, we recommend that no proposals for superstores or other large retail developments in or around market towns should be considered, unless they are accompanied by a comprehensive study of the possible retail effects over the whole of each proposal catchment area". (HMSO, 1994).

2.31   The Committee recognised that while locating a superstore in a small town centre may have an adverse impact on specialist food stores which are important to the vitality and viability of the town centre, a policy of under-providing the town centre may result in shoppers travelling to other towns. The committee identified the need to ascertain how new food superstores have competed with food shops in town centres or in local district centres. The committee was also concerned about superstores extending their product ranges to include facilities such as pharmacies and post offices.

2.32   In its response to the Fourth Report from the House of Commons Environment Select Committee, *Shopping Centres and Their Future*, published in February 1995, the Government accepted that there is a need for a greater awareness of the range of impacts of out-of-centre development. Consultation Draft PPG6, published in July 1995, stated:-

"Large food stores and supermarkets often play a vital role as anchor store in maintaining the quality and range of shopping in smaller towns and district centres. They are also essential for the less mobile of the community". (DoE, 1995).

2.33   The Government recognised that the range of goods sold at retail outlets, including large food stores/superstores, may impact on the vitality and viability of town centres and local centres. It concluded that the imposition of restrictions

should be assessed on a case by case basis, and facilities such as post offices should be retained in existing centres.

2.34   The Revised PPG6 was published in June 1996 and embodies many of the provisions of the earlier Consultation Draft. In particular, the sequential approach places the onus on developers to demonstrate that all potential town centre options have been assessed if less central locations are being proposed for development.

2.35   PPG6 also provides specific guidance for the application of the sequential approach to small and historic towns. It states that:-

"Not all centres, particularly small and historic towns, will have sites that are suitable in terms of size, parking, traffic generation or servicing arrangements for large-scale developments in the town centre itself. In such centres, developments should be of a scale appropriate to the size of the centre". (HMSO, 1996)

2.36   The Environment Select Committee has more recently reaffirmed its concern as developers turn their attention to smaller towns. In its March 1997 Report, the Chairman of the Committee stated:-

"That small and historic market towns are, by their very nature, unlikely to be possessed of town centre sites which can accommodate a modern supermarket with associated parking facilities.

A second concern, which leads on from the first, is that shopping centres in smaller towns, serving a modest population but perhaps drawing much of their trade from neighbouring settlements, will be less robust and less able to survive competition from out-of-town development. The retail impact on such towns might be severe and the vitality and viability of their centres might suffer." (HMSO, 1997)

2.37   The Committee has recommended to the Government that full impact studies should accompany all applications for significant retail development, particularly in or around small or market towns. The Government's formal response, published in July 1997, states that advice in PPG6 already recognises that impact assessments may be necessary for retail developments below 2,500m^2 gross where they could have a significant impact on a small centre, such as market towns. It also states that the research undertaken in this study should assist in providing additional guidance on the most appropriate form of impact assessment, and how impact on such centres should be interpreted.

2.38   The threats facing market towns have prompted a number of initiatives from interest groups. Some of these are considered below.

Competitive Responses

2.39   *Vital and Viable Town Centres* revealed that only 3% of planning officers in market towns described their towns as vibrant, compared with over 30% in cities. This apparent spiral of decline was, at least partly, attributed to market towns susceptibility to out-of-town food retailing:-

"In many centres, specialist food shops, such as fishmongers, have closed and there has been a considerable growth in what are perceived as "non-shops", such as building society branches, on the high street". (DoE, 1994)

2.40   The decline in the number of specialist and independent food retailers is a national trend, and one which to some extent predates the significant growth in food superstores.

2.41   *Vital and Viable Centres* identified that those market towns which are vibrant or improving are most likely to have:-

- Drawn up a profile to establish what kind of town they are, and what competition is;

- Agreed a vision of what the town centre should be;

- Drawn up strategies to set priorities and attract resources;

- Adopted programmes for encouraging markets and cafes; and

- Put a town centre management plan into practice.

2.42   According to a joint report by Donaldsons and Healey & Baker, entitled the *Effectiveness of Town Centre Management* (1994), Town Centre Management is now widely recognised as making a significant contribution to the vitality and viability of town centres. This argues that the flood of out-of-town retail facilities acted as a catalyst to the adoption of the model of shopping centre management.

2.43   According to this study, by 1994, some 80 town centre managers had been appointed. Whilst this number has now grown to in excess of 200, the House of Commons Environment Select Committee expressed recently some concern at the fact that not all towns have a Management Scheme, and some of those that do still appear to be struggling. (DoE, 1997)

2.44   Although Town Centre Management is not targeted specifically at market towns, it does nonetheless have particular relevance to the issues facing market towns. It can provide the forum in which traditional features of market towns can be exploited. Such features, according to the Rural Development Commission include:-

- Retail development in selected locations, including comparison and specialist shopping;

- Inward investment;

- Small business growth;

- Tourism promotion through community action; and

- Housing expansion and sustainable development.

2.45   Guidance on developing a town centre management strategy was provided in *Caring for our Towns and Cities* by Boots The Chemist and the Civic Trust Regeneration Unit. (1994). It stressed that town centre revitalisation requires the effective partnership of public, private and voluntary sectors. It argued that better management leads to new investment and this in turn provides an opportunity for town centres to compete against out-of-town retail facilities.

2.46   As a direct consequence of out-of-town superstores, some market towns have set up initiatives to combat the perceived threat. These include the 'Loyal To Leominster' campaign which is a collective approach on the part of retailers to encourage shoppers back to the town centre through the use of a Town Centre 'Loyalty Card'. By the end of the first month of the scheme, it had attracted 93 retailers. Indications are that at least 25% of participating retailers experienced a significant improvement in their turnover. The challenge for this and other comparable schemes elsewhere is to maintain retailers' interest and direct involvement. Leominster is one of the case studies described later in this report.

Impact Methodology

2.47   In their literature review entitled *The Effects of Major Out-of-Town Retail Developments* (1994), BDP Planning and the Oxford Institute of Retail Management suggested that the term 'retail impact' has a very wide range of interpretations, although much of the existing literature deals with the term in a very limited sense.

2.48   In general, retail impact assessments have concentrated on the calculation of diversion of trade from an existing centre or centres to a new development. However, a report of seminar proceedings undertaken by the Unit for Retail Planning Information (URPI) described the calculation of diversion from competing centres as the final stage of the analysis in existing methods (URPI, 1983). This highlighted the need for assessments to translate trade diversion into the likely effects on shops and shoppers.

2.49   The advent of the term 'vitality and viability', now embodied in PPG6, has given local authorities a sharper focus for assessing retail impact, not simply in terms of the trade diversion, but through identifying the effects on the health of town centres. PPG6 (Revised) highlights the importance of local authorities undertaking regular surveys, and being aware of other factors including retailers intentions and shopper attitudes, as well as monitoring property market indicators e.g. rents, yields and vacancy rates.

2.50   The BDP/OXIRM report summarised the available literature on retail impact in terms of economic impact, social impact and environmental impact. On the effect of large food stores on market towns, the report simply states:-

"Concern with the effects of grocery superstore development upon smaller or historic towns were also present during the 1980's (Lee Donaldson Associates, 1991). We might expect the maintenance of diversity within smaller town centres to be more problematic given a greater reliance upon convenience spending". (BDP, 1994).

2.51   This reflects the scarcity of research into the particular concerns of market towns. Whilst some indications of predicted impact are included in Consultants' reports, much of the evidence of actual 'post-opening' impact tends to be based on anecdotal evidence, rather than comprehensive 'before and after' assessments of effect of large food stores. The Government in its formal response to the Environment Committee Report on Shopping Centres, published in July 1997, confirmed its commitment to the need to improve the standard of impact studies by improving the methodology, and making them more transparent.

2.52   The use of surveys for quantitative modelling has become increasingly common amongst practitioners. However, it is less usual for local authorities, either on their own or through consultants, to undertake post-opening surveys to assess whether the predicted level of impact, both in terms of trade diversion and the effects on health of the town centre, were accurate.

2.53   The fact that retail impact methodologies vary quite considerably, and are dependent upon on a range of variables (assessment of catchment areas, population projections and expenditure growth rates), has led a number of Inspectors at Public Inquiries to question to the validity of retail impact analyses. This was highlighted at a Public Inquiry in 1994 concerning planning permission for an edge-of-centre food superstore in Cirencester, where the predicted level of impact varied significantly depending on whether a business basis or goods basis of calculation was used. The Inspector concluded:-

"If a food store were built on the appeal site, then the actual expenditure diverted to it from existing retailers would be the same whichever way it was calculated. Perhaps the point does no more than highlight the imprecise nature of retail impact estimation". (Appeal Reference T\APP\F1610\A\94\235446).

2.54   In 1992, the Scottish Office published a report by Drivers Jonas entitled *Retail Impact Assessment Methodologies*. The Scottish Office commissioned the study to examine the effectiveness of common approaches to retail impact assessments, and to identify key elements which might form the basis of an optimum method of assessment.

2.55   The study acknowledged that whilst there is little dispute amongst practitioners as to the stages in calculating percentage impact, there are a number of deficiencies in the approach. The study identified the following elements of what might be described as a conventional 'step by step' retail impact study:-

- identify study and/or catchment area;

- estimate expenditure within study and/or catchment area;

- estimate turnover of existing shopping centres;

- estimate turnover of new retail proposal;

- estimate the amount of spending in each existing centre which will be diverted to make up the new store's turnover; and

- express the amount of diverted trade from each shopping centre as a percentage of estimated pre-impact turnover of that centre.

2.56   Some of the key deficiencies identified by the consultants included:-

- lack of attempt to analyse the current shopping patterns of an area and the strengths and weaknesses of existing centres when predicting future changes;

- Practitioners often do not provide a detailed explanation of their assumptions in the apportionment of trade diversion;

- lack of attempt to establish a relationship between available expenditure and potential turnover;

- the interpretation of impact estimates is often cursory and still pre-occupied with misleading indicators such as the "10% rule";

- insufficient attention is paid to residual (post-impact) turnover estimates and to the level of reliance of a shopping centre on a particular type of shopping trip;

- assumptions about likely store closures are often unjustified;

- the probable functional relationship between a new retail development and existing centres should be examined in more detail; and

- disputes about data can undermine confidence in retail impact assessments, and often can be avoided through negotiation.

2.57   The report suggested that action was required in three key areas: policy context, quantitative assessment and interpretation. In terms of quantitative assessment, the study suggests that:-

"Retail impact assessments should be accurate with limited sensitivity, thorough, consistent, and capable of agreement between parties. Local planning authorities should make available to consultants all data held by the authority which is likely to be of assistance to the consultant in undertaking a retail impact assessment." (Scottish Office, 1992)

2.58   The report concluded that when interpreting the results of an impact assessment, the following factors need to be addressed:-

- is the existing centre fulfilling an important function in providing services and facilities for the community?

- How is it performing now (i.e. reference to estimated turnover, levels of congestion, parking, pedestrian flows, rents, etc.)?; and

- is the centre improving or declining?

2.59   Having assessed the existing conditions, the impact assessment needs to clearly identify the effects of the new development. The study identified a checklist of factors, including:-

- whether there are particular retailers who perform a vital anchor function in the centre, and who might close as a result of the new development;

- if closures do occur, what are the prospects for re-occupation by other retailers;

- Are there committed developments for other investment which would be unlikely to take place if the proposed development proceeds; and

- will the new development result in an overall improvement to the range and quality of shopping facilities in the area.

2.60   Although the Drivers Jonas report was published six years ago, a number of the issues raised, particularly in terms of the interpretation of quantitative assessments, still remain valid. In the case of market towns and district centres where issues of impact are invariably finely-balanced, this highlights the need to ensure that, wherever possible, an agreed methodology is universally applied, and clear guidelines are followed as to how results should be interpreted.

2.61   The report recognised the need for impact assessments to take account of the long-term effects. This also reflects the concern at the cumulative impact of a series of developments over time as illustrated at a Public Inquiry in Fylde in 1995 (Appeal Reference APP\M2325\A95\256459\P2). The Inspector concluded that in respect of St Anne's the opening of either of the two foodstore proposals considered at the Inquiry would adversely affect the town, and that to assess fully the consequences it is necessary to take a long-term view of, say, ten years.

2.62   The Drivers Jonas report identified the lack of centrally held data on floorspace areas, turnover and shopping patterns. The lack of this comprehensive data provision remains a key concern.

Retail Impact

(a)   Impact of Foodstores on Market Towns

2.63   The Fourth Report from the Select Committee on 'Shopping Centres and their Future' expressed longstanding concerns about the particular vulnerability of market towns to large food stores. Market towns still rely to a large extent on food shopping for their trade. Any diminution in this provision can, adversely affect their vitality and viability. This includes the important 'top-up' trade of smaller town centre stores:-

"It is the secondary top-up food shopping that is seen as vital for the linked durable shopping in market towns". (Parker, 1995).

2.64   The potential harm caused by out-of-town food stores is not necessarily limited to town centre food retailers. It is argued that durable goods retailers may suffer reduced turnover as a result of out-of-town food stores.

2.65   There is very little literature which addresses the specific concerns of market towns, although there has been research into the more general concept of retail impact. Early commentaries on the effects of superstores on towns were couched in very general terms. For example in 1976 Wade concluded that:-

"All the evidence so far available suggests that the effect of superstores and hypermarkets is dispersed across a wide area and hence a large number of stores".

2.66   Seale (1977) argued that:-

"The studies show that when a hypermarket or superstore opens, food shops in the catchment area do experience loss of turnover, actual or relative to the increase that might have been expected on the basis of national trends".

2.67   The study, 'Two of a Kind' by Derbyshire County Council (1983), attempted to compare and contrast the operations and impact of a town centre and an out-of-town superstore. It concluded that:-

"Most of the differences stem directly from the different store locations which have resulted in contrasting

patterns of mode of travel, frequency of visit, customer origin, transaction size and age/sex structure of shoppers". (Derbyshire County Council, 1983).

2.68   The study concluded that the turnover level of the out-of-town Asda was significantly higher than the town centre Morrisons. Not surprisingly, the proportion of locally derived turnover is greater at Morrisons than at Asda, and the proportion of car-borne turnover was greater at Asda (out-of-town superstore) than at Morrisons.

2.69   In terms of the impact of the food superstores upon existing shopping centres, the study concluded that it was perhaps too early to be conclusive, but there were indications that there had been a wide dispersal of impact with the largest single concentration being upon Staveley itself (i.e. the location of the town centre Morrisons superstore).

2.70   In BDP and OXIRM's Literature Review on the effects of out-of-town retail development they referred to Lee Donaldson's 1991 study which concluded that despite the growth of superstores, no authority had been able to demonstrate on the basis of survey data that a superstore would have a severe adverse affect in terms of the scale, structure and diversity of town centres.

(b)   Post PPG6 (Revised) (July 1993)

2.71   Since 1993 and the advent of PPG6, the interpretation of retail impact has been broadened beyond trade diversion, to include wider considerations of the impact on vitality and viability. As a consequence, greater weight has been attached to retail impact in its wider sense, and this has been reflected in Public Inquiries.

2.72   For example, at the Public Inquiry in Fylde in 1995, the Inspector concluded that the proposed developments *"would each be likely to harm the vitality and viability of St Annes town centre and they would each, therefore, be contrary to the adopted Local Plan"*. The particular concern in this case was the likely impact on the town centre Safeway, which the Inspector considered on balance of probability would close.

2.73   There is no commonly accepted level of impact which is considered either acceptable or unacceptable. This will vary depending on the size, function, and relative health of each town centre under consideration. In the Inspector's Decision Letter, following a Public Inquiry into non-determination of a planning application for an edge-of-centre superstore in Cirencester, he stated that notwithstanding his concerns over the calculation of the impact figure:-

"It shows a diversion of convenience goods expenditure to the proposed store of about 11%, not normally a high enough proportion to suggest a harmful effect on vitality and viability". (Planning Inspectorate, 1994)

2.74   In the case of small market towns, the level of impact which is likely to be acceptable will, in general, be less than for larger towns. This sentiment was clearly expressed by the Inspector at a Public Inquiry into two planning applications for large food stores in Ludlow. He stated that:-

"it is with some concern that I contemplate the possibility of convenience trade of between 28% and 45% being diverted from the town centre as a result of one or other of the proposed stores being built…

Ludlow is only a small market town with a thinly populated catchment area and it seems to me that, with the levels of impact forecast for each of the stores (between 28% and 45% diversion of trade from the town centre), if PPG6 harm could occur anywhere at all it could happen in this town". (Planning Inspectorate, 1994).

2.75   An Inquiry in 1996 in Southwell in Nottinghamshire considered two out-of-centre Co-op supermarket proposals. The Inspector concluded that either of the individual proposals would have a detrimental effect on Southwell town centre. He considered that Southwell was a vulnerable centre which relied heavily on its convenience shopping role, and whilst vacancy levels were well below the national average, the potential loss of two of the remaining six convenience stores in the centre would be unacceptable. In his decision letter he stated:

"In assessing retail impact there is inevitably a measure of speculation about the effects of additional shopping floorspace. In the case of Southwell, however, the need to preserve the vitality and viability of this unique and attractive market town must give extra weight to the risks represented by out-of-centre retail development."
(Refs:APP/U/A/95/260811 and EMP 3030/220/15)

2.76   Similarly, a strict interpretation of PPG6 was employed at a Public Inquiry in Porthmadoc in May 1997 into refusal of outline planning permission for an out-of-centre Tesco "Compact" supermarket. Whilst the Inspector concluded that Porthmadoc town centre was vital and viable, and the proposed Tesco would represent an improvement in the quality of shopping presently in the town, he considered that the store would have an unacceptable impact on the town centre. In his decision letter he stated:

"In my judgement therefore, if this out-of-centre supermarket were built, the direct loss of trade coupled with the attraction of shoppers out-of-centre would lead to the closure of the main supermarket in the shopping centre and a considerable contraction in the rest of the convenience sector.

The vitality of the centre would suffer as a consequence and I consider that the combination of loss of shoppers from the town centre and the competition from the new supermarket would lead to the closure of some of the existing small food shops… A larger shopping centre could absorb such closures but, in a centre as small as this, the consequent reduction in variety and choice would be marked."
(Appeal Ref: T/APP/Q6810/A/97/510480)

2.77   In contrast at Street, in Somerset, the Secretary of State granted planning permission for an edge-of-centre superstore, reflecting the particular circumstances of the town:-

"He agrees that as a market town, Street has a thriving, singular and unique trading character, not anchored by food retailing and he is satisfied that the scheme will not affect the vitality and viability of Street and Glastonbury town centres as a whole".
(Ref: SW/P/5363/220/3)

2.78   These cases show clearly that no two market towns are alike. As a consequence, it is not possible to generalise about the likely impact of large food stores. However, a principal consideration is the level of food store provision in the town centre, and the extent to which this serves to underpin the vitality and viability of the town.

2.79   Research undertaken by Somerfield, entitled 'Backing Britain's High Streets' (1994) and prepared as a Memorandum of Evidence to the House of Commons Select Committee, included 10 case studies of towns affected by out-of-town food store developments. These covered a wide spectrum of towns, both in terms of size and geographical location.

2.80   In each case study, evidence was put forward to suggest that the town centres had suffered increased vacancies, and an increase in the proportion of service uses, a deterioration in the quality and range of retailing, and a reduction in retail turnover. However, there was no attempt to determine whether any of these adverse 'impacts' were attributable to other factors apart from the out-of-town developments, not least the recent economic recession. This comprehensive assessment of impact is generally lacking from most of the available literature.

2.81   In 1997 Rapleys published a study on behalf of Safeway Stores Plc to examine the changes in the mix of retail uses in six market towns where Safeway foodstores had opened recently. These include Market Drayton, Totnes, Fakenham, Liskeard, Rushden and Tavistock. The six towns, with the exception of Rushden, are small market towns with populations of below 10,000. In addition, Rapleys analysed two market towns which had not been subject to any new foodstore development since 1990 (Ludlow and Amesbury). These provided a control against which the other six market towns could be assessed.

2.82   We have included Fakenham as one of our case study towns; the results and implications of which are considered in Chapter six. Our own more comprehensive assessment has highlighted some of the limitations of the analysis undertaken by Rapleys. In particular, the study did not attempt to measure any retail impact arising from the edge-of-centre/out-of-centre foodstores, but to concentrate on three of the vitality and viability indicators set out in Figure 1 of PPG6; the diversity of uses; retailer representation; and the proportion of vacant street level property.

2.83   The key findings of the study were:-

- *the opening of new foodstores in these centres has not had any marked effect on the national trend towards a decline in convenience retailing from small shops or in the total number or proportion of vacant street level premises in the town centres nearest to the new stores;*

- *comparison between the towns with edge-of-centre stores and towns with out-of-centre stores shows that the rate of change in the representation of convenience units is not very different;*

- *the general changes in the composition of all the centres surveyed are consistent with UK average trends, indicating that wider social and economic influences are the main factor affecting the mix of uses and level of vacancies. This is reflected, for instance, in the rate of change in butcher's shops in Ludlow (with no new foodstore), which lost 40% (2 out of 5) of its butchers during the study period.*

- *the analysis of service and durable unit representation in towns with edge-of-centre and out-of-centre stores shows that there is no significant difference in the rate of change."* (Rapleys, 1997)

2.84   Whilst this research provides some insight into the effects of large foodstores on market towns and attempts to place these in the context of the recent economic recession, it only addresses three vitality and viability indicators and does not measure the long term consequences of foodstore development.

Employment Impact

2.85   There has been no concerted attempt to date to assess the impact of superstores on local retail employment in market towns and district centres. What little research has been undertaken has tended to concentrate on wider national trends, rather than on the specific circumstances of individual centres. This reflects both the

difficulties of obtaining accurate and sufficiently disaggregated employment data at a local level, and also attributing cause and effect.

2.86   In an attempt to address some of the principal difficulties in analysing changes in employment, as a result of superstores, Boots has recently undertaken a study on behalf of the National Retail Planning Forum, entitled *The Impact of Out-of-Centre Food Superstores on Local Retail Employment* (1998). Whilst not specifically aimed at market towns and district centres, the Study attempts to analyse changes in local retail employment between 1991 and 1995, using 5km, 10km and 15km catchment areas of 93 superstores which opened during this period.

2.87   The key findings of the research are:-

- there is strong evidence that new food superstores have on average, a negative effect on retail employment;

- Within the 15km catchment areas of the 93 superstores, employment in specialist food retailers declined by -24,988 (-29.4%), offsetting the 10,419 (+5.4%) increase in full-time equivalents employed in the superstore sector and resulting in a net decrease of -14,569 full-time equivalent (-5.2%) in the overall food retailing sector;

- There was also a decline in non-food retail employment of 1.7%, resulting in a decline in total retail employment of 2.9%;

- The net impact of the 93 superstore openings is estimated to be a reduction of full-time equivalent employees of 3%; and

- Each superstore opening resulted in an average net loss in employment of -276 full-time equivalents.

2.88   Superstore operators, on the other hand, highlight the significant contribution large foodstores can make to local employment, providing a range of full time and flexible part time employment which may be well suited to local needs.

Transport Issues

2.89   In 1990 the government identified the transportation issues raised by superstore development in 'This Common Inheritance':-

"Out-of-town shopping can be inaccessible to the least mobile people, including the old; it can lengthen car journeys; and it can sometimes threaten the town centre economy". (HMSO, 1990)

2.90   The Environment Committee Fourth Report *Shopping Centres and Their Future* states:-

"The Government's long term objective, as put forward in its Sustainable Development Strategy, is to encourage the reduction in the rate of increase of car usage, because car usage otherwise would make it virtually impossible to meet our international commitments on pollution. In the case of some shopping trips, this will be problematic. Bulk food shopping, for example, is at present only practicable by car, as is shopping for heavy DIY items". (HMSO, 1994)

2.91   The government objectives have been translated into policy primarily within PPG13 and PPG6 the focus of which, in respect of food shopping, is to preferably locate new superstores in town centres where people can park and then use other town centre facilities.

2.92   Very few, if any, of the publications on travel patterns to superstores focus on market towns or district centres. Most deal with the issue in a more general sense, and if anything concentrate more on well established urban centres. This is probably because this has been the area of main development by the superstore operators over the last 10 to 15 years. In addition, the majority of the research on the subject has been sponsored or undertaken by the food operators themselves, although this is no indication that the results are any less robust and they should be given due regard in the debate. Perhaps the most informative source of background information on travel patterns is the National Travel Survey which deals with travel for all purposes not just food shopping.

2.93   The Environment Committee was somewhat dismissive of research into CO_2 emissions due to food shopping stating:-

"Various arguments on CO_2 emissions were presented to us. For example, it was suggested that providing new out-of-town superstores reduces the length of shopping trips and therefore CO_2 emissions. Another argument was that more town centre development would lead to additional town centre traffic and therefore increased emissions from longer journey times and lower vehicle operating efficiency. We regard such arguments as baseless. There has simply not been sufficient independent research to warrant any claims about the relationship between shopping patterns and CO_2 emissions. This is serious since policies for sustainable development are being made in the absence of any knowledge about how sustainability is quantified". (HMSO, 1994)

2.94   It is worth setting the issue in context. Research sponsored by J Sainsbury entitled *Food Shopping and the Car*, shows that food shopping accounts for around 2.5% of total household car mileage.

2.95   The research referred to in this section is not specific to market towns. However much of it is applicable, to an extent, and the issues it raises are certainly the ones on which we need to focus.

2.96   The key issues in this area of debate can be summarised as follows:

- The effect on travel distance and frequency due to opening of a new store;

- Linking or combining of trips ie food with non-food, leisure etc;

- Modal Split; and

- Congestion effects.

2.97   The hypotheses commonly put forward by the main superstore operators in publications and at public inquiries can be summarised as follows:-

- introduction of a new superstore within a town will actually reduce trip lengths and overall travel distance. This is due to the fact that, in the main, people will travel to their nearest store. Therefore the more stores there are the shorter will be the required travel distance;

- introduction of a modern superstore close to a town will draw back food shopping (and, as a consequence, possible non-food shopping) that is currently leaking to other stores and towns further away;

- town centre and edge-of-centre foodstores encourage more people to enter the town by car to undertake bulk food shopping. This has a detrimental effect on the town centre environment.

2.98   Evidence from Tesco is contained within *PPG13 Applied to Retail Development: The Minimisation of Carbon Dioxide and other Polluting Emissions* prepared by RPS Nigel Moor for Tesco. The report states:

"Tesco's site research department has shown that for eleven freestanding towns the average miles travelled to the supermarket was better than halved after the new superstore was opened. The average reduction per store was approximately 60,000 miles per week which equates to 3 million miles annually". (RPS Nigel Moor, 1994)

2.99   The research referred to is unpublished but the report goes on to quote a specific example in Twickenham where a new Tesco is contended to have reduced the total distance travelled for shopping by circa 20%.

2.100   Further evidence to support this hypothesis is provided in *Superstore Impact on Travel Patterns* prepared for J Sainsbury by the Transport Studies Unit at Oxford University. The research was based on home interviews and travel diaries and investigated Swindon, where two new superstores (a Tesco and a Sainsbury) had recently opened although the research concentrated on the impact of the Sainsbury. Some of the key results were as follows:

"Overall, the total number of car food shopping trips rose by 3.5%, but the average distance fell by 9.3%, giving a total distance travelled by car for food shopping falling by 6.2%".

2.101   Safeway commissioned research which was partly funded by TRICS and reported in *Traffic and Parking at Food Retailing – TRICS Report 95/3*. The impact of the opening of 6 stores was investigated, the stores being either town centre or within the built up area. The results suggest a range of travel distance savings between 29% and 54% with only one store showing a projected increase.

2.102   The results referred to above appear to show support for the contention that provision of a new store within a mature area of food shopping will lead to reduced travel distance for food shopping. However, the methodologies vary and are not always fully reported, and it should be remembered that the research is not specific to market towns.

2.103   Perhaps the main point of discussion over these results is whether they look at a sufficiently broad picture. This leads to the question of combining or linking trips. An area of debate is the extent to which trips for food shopping are combined with other shopping or other activities within the town. For example, if there is currently significant linking of trips by those using an existing town centre food store, and if these people then transfer to a new out-of-town/edge-of-town store, they may instead make a series of separate, new trips; a one stop trip to the new foodstore and a separate trip to the town centre for comparison shopping. Thus the overall change in travel distance may be different to the change due to food shopping alone. There is very little research on this subject.

2.104   One contention is that the degree of linkage is so small as to be insignificant. The Environment Committee reported:-

"There appears to be unwarranted scepticism of encouraging combined shopping trips among the major food retailers. We recommend that planning policy guidance be amended, to include a presumption that superstores are best located in or on the edge-of-town centres unless there are very strong indications to the contrary. We believe that implementation of such a policy should help to reduce car journeys, as well as giving shoppers the opportunity to combine food and non-food shopping trips". (HMSO, 1994)

2.105 The Safeway/TRICS report shows the proportion of customers who used 'other local facilities' when carrying out food shopping that did not involve moving a parked car. For town centre stores the average varies between 46% and 56% depending upon the time period but excluding Sundays. For out-of-centre stores the average varies from 16% to 24%.

2.106 However in the report *Food Shopping and the Car* undertaken by Telephone Surveys for J Sainsbury, only 11% of those using town centre or edge-of-centre stores regularly combined food shopping with shopping for durable goods. The surveys were based on 7000 telephone surveys of both car and non car shoppers.

2.107 Turning to the issue of modal choice, it seems that if people have a car available for food shopping they will use it. A report entitled *Car Dependence* from the RAC Foundation for Motoring and the Environment concludes that:-

"A very large proportion of car owners have established a very strong pattern to do their main bulk food shopping on a weekly basis, by car, to a reasonably close supermarket. The distances involved are not such as to make it impossible for public transport to compete – and even walking for a significant proportion – rather, the dominant influence is simply carrying the goods. In this activity, what has happened is that private cars have in effect become a freight delivery system, the last link in the chain from factory to home.

Cairns (1995) suggests that the only radical alternative to the idea of weekly food shopping by car is the development of home delivery services and the creation of a network of neighbourhood shops which act as distribution agents for the quality and range of goods available at supermarkets."

2.108 The national figures taken from the *Food Shopping and the Car* report show 99.6% of those with a car available for the main food shop use it. In Witney 92% of food shopping was undertaken by car in spite of the same proportion (92%) of shopping destinations being within the town centre. This Oxfordshire data also suggests that the average travel distance to a foodstore is similar whether the store is in or out of town. Of those who do not have a car available some 30% use a car for food shopping through obtaining a lift or a taxi.

2.109 The RAC report quoting Headicar and Curtis (1995) suggests that culture plays a role in modal and other choices:

"There seem to be different cultures prevailing amongst the surveyed populations which predispose people to different preferred behaviour". (ibid)

2.110 Finally, there is the question of the congestion effects of locating foodstores in town centres or on the edge-of-centres. There are two main issues. First, the level of polluting emissions (in addition to CO^2) depends upon road type, speed etc. The contention is that encouraging food store development in town centres encourages more traffic into those locations producing more harmful emissions than if trips were undertaken to a foodstore on the edge or out-of-town. Second, there is the view that one does not wish to encourage more traffic into congested town centres due to delays to other road users, pressure on car parking etc.

2.111 Nigel Moor in his report states:-

"The option suggested in PPG6 for edge-of-centre development is justified for its perceived benefits to non car owners and to the town centre strategy, but it may not be the best solution in environmental terms. It is important that the environmental impacts related to air quality are considered. Where an out-of-centre site is likely to have less impact, this factor should be weighted accordingly". (RPS Nigel Moor, 1994)

2.112 One of the key factors affecting the impact on town centre traffic of a new store will be the degree of linking of trips that takes place. If people already regularly combine food and non food shopping in the town centre then the addition (or retention) of a foodstore in the centre may have little impact. Conversely, if combined trips are few and far between and people currently make separate trips into the town centre for food and non food shopping, transfer of some of the food trips to an out-of-centre location may have advantages (provided people still return to the town centre to do their comparison shopping).

2.113 This is an issue that has particular relevance for market towns and where research based on larger towns may be less relevant. This is due to the more constrained nature of many market towns and the concentration of shopping activity in one centre rather than in a series of suburban or district centres.

2.114 The methodologies currently used to assess the suitability in transport terms of a location for superstore development have three primary facets:-

- The changes in car travel distance as a result of the new store;

- The accessibility of the store by public transport (primarily bus); and

- The accessibility of the store by walk and cycle modes.

2.115 There is no accepted or formally published guidance on methodology. The *Guidelines for Traffic Impact Assessment* published by the Institution of Highways and Transportation in 1994 were formulated before many of the issues now before us were to the fore, and therefore offers very little assistance. Therefore, the methodologies have been derived by practitioners as they have considered individual store proposals. Whilst this inevitably leads to differences in approach, there does seem to be some consensus over the general methodology to be adopted, although important differences do occur. Some variation in approach is perhaps healthy since different sites and proposals will need different scales and types of study.

2.116 The generalised approach to assessing the changes in travel patterns is described by Mayer and Mynors in papers presented to the 1995 TRICS conference. This is similar to the approach adopted by Savell Bird and Axon for studies in Fylde, Hull, Hedge End and elsewhere. The approach builds on surveys of shoppers within the catchment area and the retail impact study which will provide information on the geographical areas (zones) from which trade to the new store will be derived. The distance to the existing store used and to the new store from each zone is measured in order to determine the change in travel distance. Decisions need to be made on the size of zone (in theory, one house is the smallest zone possible but often postcodes or enumeration districts are used) and whether to measure distances 'as the crow flies' or along actual roads. Clearly, the greater the sophistication and detail the greater will be the cost.

2.117 However this approach may be of insufficient detail in some instances and may need to be refined as a result of other important factors such as:-

(a) the change in frequency due to people visiting a new and probably closer store more often;

(b) the effect of combined trips, i.e. changes in the relationship between food and comparison shopping brought about by the new store;

(c) the effect of linked trips, e.g. trips, from work to store to home. These factors are difficult to measure and thus are often ignored. One problem is that one does not know the relative importance of the factors until they have been assessed; and

(d) the type of road used, e.g. congested or free flowing.

2.118 Mayer at TRICS 1995 stated:-

"For a superstore from our experience the journey saving calculation will usually show a saving of up to about 10 million vehicle kilometres per year, depending on relative locations. This sounds impressive but usually represents a relatively small percentage saving in journeys to superstores in the area as a whole".

2.119 In fact it is unlikely that rules of thumb can be derived to show the expected savings due to the variations between locations. Furthermore, since the changes are, in most cases, a small percentage of the total distance travelled to superstores, a change in some of the key variables can have a significant effect on the result of the analysis.

2.120 A number of methodologies have been developed to assess the accessibility of a location by public transport and, in particular, by bus. Some of these are usefully summarised in papers presented to a conference entitled *Providing Development with Multi Modal Access* organised by the University of Westminster on 27 October 1995. The London Borough of Hammersmith and Fulham have developed perhaps the most detailed methodology which takes account of walk times frequency and reliability of services. These factors are assessed to give a Public Transport Accessibility Level (PTAL) for different sites and areas within the borough. However this system has been developed for London boroughs with dense population and numerous different public transport routes and services. The method needs some adaptation for use within market towns.

2.121 Other methodologies are similar in basic concept, but include various developments and differences in detail. One of the most important developments is the application of Geographical Information Systems (GIS) to assist in the presentation of data.

2.122 The key issue in determining the accessibility by walk and cycle modes is the distance it is reasonable to expect people to walk/cycle with shopping. This may not be straight forward since the volume of shopping purchased during each trip may itself be determined by the mode. Therefore someone who chooses to walk to a superstore will only buy as much food as they can reasonably carry home. This person is therefore not undertaking the traditional weekly bulk food shop but rather a series of smaller purchases. A recent literature review undertaken by ETP for the National Retail Planning Forum on accessibility, walking and linked trips has confirmed that there is a relative lack of information on the subject.

Summary

2.123 Our literature review has highlighted some of the difficulties in defining precisely what constitutes a market town or district centre. Both references are used in common parlance but are often used as generic terms to encompass a wide diversity of small towns/centres.

2.124 Work undertaken on behalf of the DoE (*Vital and Viable Town Centres: Meeting the Challenge*), and more recently by the Rural Development Commission has provided a clearer focus on the key features of market towns; their changing role; and the principal challenges facing them. In contrast, relatively little has been written about district centres, and the challenges facing them are less well defined.

2.125 Despite the problems of definition, it is clear that both market towns and district centres rely to a large extent on convenience retailing to underpin their economic vitality and viability. As such, the focus of this study, to assess the impact of large foodstores, is equally relevant to both.

2.126 There is a degree of consensus about the most appropriate method of assessing impact; namely a 'step by step approach'. However, there are important deficiencies. These include insufficient explanations of assumptions used; cursory interpretation of impact estimates; and failure to agree key data inputs. The importance of accurate data on floorspace areas, turnover and shopping patterns cannot be overestimated.

2.127 There is more empirical research data on transport issues, mainly undertaken by or sponsored by the major retailers. This has tended to concentrate on specific issues, such as travel distance. There is less information available on use of superstores by non car modes which currently forms the minority of users of freestanding superstores. Very little, if any, of the research has been aimed specifically at market towns; a problem which is not confined just to transport issues. There is an emerging methodology for assessing predicted changes in travel distance as a result of a new superstore, but there are important differences of approach between practitioners.

CHAPTER 3
Local Authority Views

Overview of Local Authority Attitudes

3.1 A postal survey of all local authorities in England and Wales was undertaken in February 1996 to identify those market towns and district centres which have experienced the development of large food stores with a gross floorspace of more than 2,500 m² (26,900 ft²) since 1985. The survey covered a total of 416 local authorities, including Metropolitan Boroughs and County Councils.

3.2 The key issues addressed by the survey include:-

- Whether local authorities are facing pressure for further food superstore development, and if so, for what type of location (town centre/edge-of-centre/out-of-centre);

- Whether local authorities require retail impact assessments when considering applications for new food store developments, and if so whether this includes proposals for town centre and edge-of-centre locations;

- The approach local authorities propose adopting to assess the impact of proposals in terms of retail impact, accessibility, travel generation, traffic generation and environmental impact;

- Whether local authorities have commissioned any post-opening surveys to assess the effects of large food stores on the vitality and viability of their market towns or district centres;

- Whether local authorities consider that they have sufficient expertise to assess the retail and transport implications of large food store proposals; and

- Whether local authorities consider that current methodologies are adequate to assess retail and transport effects of large food stores on market towns and district centres.

3.3 We received 178 responses, representing a response rate of just over 43%. Of these, approximately 54 responses were not considered directly relevant; a number of the towns specified were outside our population parameters. We also came to the conclusion in discussion with London and Metropolitan Boroughs that applying a systematic analysis of cause and effect of large food stores in many inner city areas is not a practical proposition. Therefore, we only reviewed responses from authorities where the effects of a new store on a clearly defined centre were readily identifiable.

(a) The Pressure for Further Development

3.4 Almost 54% of respondents were facing pressure for further food store development. Of those that had received a planning application(s), as opposed to just speculative interest, 56% had received one planning application; 22% had received two planning applications; and a further 22% had received more than two applications. This suggests that despite significant large food store developments nationally during the 1980's and 1990's, food operators still consider that there is significant demand for further development.

3.5 Of the 127 planning applications received, almost 28% were subsequently withdrawn; 31% were still in the process of being considered. Only 13% had been granted planning permission by the Planning Authority, although a further 11% had been granted planning permission at appeal or had been called in by the Secretary of State.

(b) Local Authority's Approach to Impact Assessment

3.6   Almost 75% of local authorities, usually require a retail impact assessment when considering applications for any new food store development. This suggests that most are following Government Planning Policy Guidance outlined in PPG6, and are having particular regard to the potential impact of foodstores on the vitality and viability of existing centres. 21% of respondents do not usually require retail impact assessments (although this percentage may be distorted somewhat by the inclusion of town centre stores).

3.7   Some 38% of respondents usually require retail impact assessments for proposals for town centre and edge-of-town locations. A further 22% consider that the need for a retail impact assessment will depend on the particular location of the proposal. 30% do not require assessments for the town centre/edge-of-centre proposals. This suggests that there is no universally accepted approach by local authorities to the requirement for retail impact assessments. However, local authorities are predominantly concerned with the impact of out-of-centre locations, and are more likely to request a retail impact assessment in the case of out-of-centre proposals.

3.8   69% of local authorities facing pressure for further food store development use external consultants to undertake retail impact assessments – only 18% undertake the analysis themselves. This contrasts to other types of impact assessment, where local authorities are more likely to undertake the work internally. For example, over half of local authorities carry out their own environmental impact assessment.

3.9   In terms of attaching weight to different types of impact, retail impact was identified by more local authorities than any other type (94%). Traffic generation and travel generation were considered equally important factors, although slightly less weight was attached to accessibility considerations and environmental impact. While local authorities are generally alive to the issue of retail impact, systematic analysts of travel generation, and the environmental and other effects of new retail development, are largely overlooked or considered to be of less significance.

(c) Post-Opening Surveys

3.10   Only 14% of local authorities had commissioned post-opening surveys, although a further 3% intended to do so. The limited number of post-opening surveys suggests that local

Town Centre Waitrose, Henley.

authorities are generally unaware of the actual impact of out-of-centre/edge-of-centre food stores on existing centres. This suggests that there is little evidence to indicate whether the methods employed in the pre-opening surveys are the most appropriate in assessing the potential effects of new food stores.

3.11   Furthermore, 73% of local authorities do not believe that they have sufficient expertise to assess the retail and transport implications of large food store proposals. Again, this highlights the specialist nature of this type of work, and local authorities perception that it is necessary to seek the advice of external consultants on this issue.

(d)   Adequacy of Current Methodologies

3.12   Almost 45% of local authorities do not consider that current methodologies for assessing retail and transport effects of large food stores are adequate. Although many authorities did not indicate specifically what they felt were the main deficiencies, a general concern expressed was that the key variables used in impact methodology could easily be manipulated to endorse a particular viewpoint. Doubts were expressed about the objectivity of many applicants' retail impact assessments.

The Impact of Individual Food Stores

3.13   As part of our Local Authority survey, we included a proforma for local authorities to complete for each store built since 1985 with a gross floorspace of 2,500 m² and over. The purpose of this was to ascertain:-

- Whether planning permission was granted by the authority or on appeal;

- What form(s) of impact assessment were undertaken by the applicant;

- Whether the Local Planning Authority commissioned any independent assessment of the proposals;

- Whether the Local Planning Authority considered that the retail impact analysis

submitted in support of the food store was adequate for reaching a clear view/decision on the likely impact of the proposal;

- Whether the applicant or local authority considered the likely effects of the food store on the overall number and length of trips undertaken by private car when determining the application; and

- The effects on nearby town centres in terms of the scale and quality of food store retailers in the centre, vacancy levels, pedestrian flows, retail development proposals, and employment levels.

3.14   To assist in identifying changes in local planning authorities' attitudes to the location of large food stores, and their propensity to undertake or require applicants to submit impact assessments, the results have been analysed for the periods between 1985 to 1990, and 1991 to 1996.

(a)   How Planning Permission was Granted

3.15   Those local authorities which completed the proformas identified a total of 154 stores of 2,500 m² gross built since 1985. Only 17.5% were town centre stores, the vast majority of which were granted planning permission by the local authority. This highlights the level of decentralisation of foodstore development since 1985, partly as a consequence of the more permissive planning policy context prior to the publication of PPG6 (Revised).

3.16   A slightly higher proportion of food stores were developed on edge-of-centre sites (21.4%). Of these, some 61% were developed between 1991 and 1996. Again, the vast majority were granted planning permission by the authority rather than on appeal.

3.17   Of those surveyed, 61% of food stores built since 1985 have been in out-of-centre locations. In contrast to the town centre and edge-of-centre locations, a much higher proportion of planning permissions were granted on appeal. This was equally true for food stores developed between 1985 and 1990 and between 1991 and 1996.

(b) Impact Studies Undertaken

3.18   No impact studies were undertaken for 82% of the town centre stores identified in our survey built between 1991 and 1996. This compares with 69% of stores built between 1985 and 1990. Of those stores which were subject to impact studies, the most common types of studies were retail impact (9%) and traffic generation studies (9%). (These percentages relate to a relatively small number of responses, and should not be regarded as a fully comprehensive cross section of town centre stores developed between 1985 and 1996).

3.19   Impact studies are undertaken most often for edge-of-centre and out-of-centre food stores. For example, retail impact studies were undertaken for 35% of edge-of-centre food stores identified in the survey, and 52% of out-of-centre stores between 1991 and 1996. However, relatively few travel and traffic generation studies were undertaken for edge-of-centre and out-of-centre stores, and no stores were subject to accessibility or environmental impact studies. Between 1991 and 1996 some 45% of edge-of-centre and 36% of out-of-centre food stores had not been subject to any form of impact study. Again, this is surprising given the change in emphasis in Government Planning Policy Guidance during this period.

3.20   Independent assessments were most frequently undertaken for out-of-centre food stores; this was particularly noticeable during the period 1991 to 1996. Nonetheless, a large percentage of local planning authorities indicated that independent assessments were not undertaken, suggesting that local authorities either carry out their own assessments, or rely upon those provided by the applicant.

(c) Adequacy of Retail Impact Assessments

3.21   Of the food stores identified, in 50% of the cases local planning authorities did not indicate whether or not they considered the analysis submitted was adequate for reaching a clear view on their likely impact. Between 1991 and 1996, 16% stated categorically that the impact analysis was inadequate. This indicates that many local authorities are sceptical about retail impact studies submitted in support of a food store proposal, or are unclear as to what the study means in terms of the likely effect on town centres.

3.22   An almost identical set of responses were identified by local authorities when asked whether the specific impact assessments submitted were adequate for making a decision. On the basis that a majority of planning applications between the period 1985 to 1996 were determined by the authorities themselves, this suggests that in some instances, decisions were being made based on inadequate or incomplete information concerning the likely retail impact on town centres.

3.23   In 65% of out-of-centre food stores developed between 1991 – 1996, no assessment of the overall effect of the store on trip lengths or the use of the private car was undertaken. None of the stores in question was subject to a thorough combined retail and transportation impact assessment.

(d) The Effect of the Store on Nearby Town Centres

3.24   Three of the total of eight town centre stores considered were believed to have had a negative impact on the scale and quality of food stores in nearby town centres. Similarly, two of town centre food stores had a detrimental impact on vacancy levels in nearby town centres. The only positive impact on nearby town centres was in respect of increased employment in retail, distribution and food preparation and processing, noted in respect of three stores.

3.25   These results suggest that notwithstanding policy preference for new food stores in town centres, local authorities have some concerns about the impact of these stores on nearby centres. This is most likely to be of concern where there are a number of smaller towns with overlapping catchment areas, and where one town's economic health is closely interlinked with another. This suggests that it may be necessary to consider the retail impact of a new town centre food store on neighbouring town centres in these circumstances. It is not only out-of-centre or edge-of-centre developments which give rise to concerns at their retail impact.

3.26   The number of responses relating to edge-of-centre developments was relatively limited (12). Many authorities felt that they did not have sufficient information to answer the question. However, responses suggest that local authorities perceive edge-of-centre food stores to have had more negative effects than positive effects on nearby town centres.

3.27   A higher response (48 in total) was achieved in respect of out-of-centre developments. Local authorities considered that 50% of these developments led to an adverse impact on the range and quality of foodstores in nearby town centres, and 31% were believed to have contributed to increased vacancy rates.

3.28   Few local authorities were prepared to venture any opinion on the effects of out-of-centre foodstores on overall car usage, the length and pattern of trips, or modal split in town centres.

Summary

3.29   The results illustrate the difficulties of reaching generalised conclusions on the basis of often very limited evidence. The survey reinforces the need for post-opening surveys, and that these need to be sufficiently rigorous to identify not only the impact on the more tangible indicators (e.g. vacancy levels and the range and quality of retailing in the town centre), but also the effect on the wider economic health of a town centre. It is clear from

the survey that many large food stores in edge-of-centre or out-of-centre locations in smaller market towns and district centres are believed to have had an adverse impact on nearby town centres.

3.30   Illustrating the consequences of the development of a large food store in one town centre for neighbouring town centres, local authorities concerns relate to town centre, as well as edge-of-centre/out-of-centre proposals. While the latter attract more criticism, and have been the subject of greater scrutiny, the other alarming conclusion to arise from our survey is the lack of consistency between authorities when considering the effects of new retail development.

3.31   Very few local authorities are entirely satisfied with current approaches to retail impact; over 20% do not usually require a retail impact assessment, yet raise concerns at the consequences of new stores. Systematic analysis of transportation effects and the accessibility of new stores on a consistent basis is almost non-existent. The findings of our survey suggest that the current study is timely, and is critical to address major deficiencies in the current level of research and expertise available to local authorities to evaluate the impact of large food stores on market towns and district centres.

CHAPTER 4
Retailer Views

4.1   Questionnaires were sent out in February 1996 with reminders in July 1996 to all the main foodstore operators. The questionnaire was designed to determine:-

- retailer store development programmes;

- future store location and catchment requirements;

- attitudes towards out-of-centre and edge-of-centre locations;

- views on the most appropriate means of measuring the impact of new stores; and

- experience to date of the impact of superstores on town centre stores, employment and investment prospects.

4.2   The response from retailers has been mixed. Whilst some have been supportive of the research and have invested some considerable time in preparing responses to the questionnaire, others have been less forthcoming, and have not been prepared to contribute to the study. Other retailers have completed parts of the questionnaire, but have either been reluctant to or unable due to lack of information to complete other elements.

4.3   Tesco and Sainsbury have provided comprehensive responses to the questionnaire, and in addition have included a wealth of detailed background data on store size and composition. Somerfield has also responded positively to the survey, and has shown clearly its commitment to the need to undertake this research. Safeway has not responded directly to our questionnaire, identifying difficulties in collating the necessary information, but has provided useful research data undertaken by Rapleys; a commentary of which is included in Section Three.

4.4   Those main foodstore operators who responded positively to the survey have, in general, also assisted in providing information on issues of turnover and impact in relation to individual case studies (e.g. Tesco, Sainsbury, Somerfield and Safeway). Similarly, Boots has provided invaluable assistance in analysing the change in turnover of its own stores in the case study towns, both prior to and after the development of the edge-of-centre/out-of-centre foodstore in question.

4.5   A number of retailers expressed some difficulty in defining what constitutes a district centre; identifying the variety of centres which perform the role of a district centre.

Number of Store Openings and Closures

4.6   Retailers were asked to identify the total number of their stores in England and Wales over 2,500 m^2 gross. They were also asked to provide details of stores in market towns and district centres which have closed since 1985, together with an indication of those market towns or district centres where they are currently actively pursuing new store developments and/or an extension to existing stores.

4.7   The representation of two of the leading superstore operators, Tesco and Sainsbury, illustrates the scale and location of superstore developments, and the changing nature of retailers' requirements.

4.8   Tesco has some 362 stores in England and Wales over 2,500 m² gross, which the company categorises as:-

32% – in centre;
18% – edge-of-centre;
50% – out-of-centre.

4.9   A total of 100 of these (28%) are located in market towns. Since 1985, Tesco has closed a total of 47 stores in market towns; 55% of which were the result of relocations to either edge-of-centre or out-of-centre stores. At the time of Tesco's response to the survey, the retailer was actively pursuing 35 proposals for new stores, and two for extensions of existing stores in market towns. These include examples of Tesco's compact store format (e.g. Princes Risborough). In total, 22 of the proposals for new stores were in out-of-centre locations, and 13 were for edge-of-centre locations.

4.10   Sainsbury currently operates some 348 stores of more than 2,500 m², which the company categorises as:-

42% – in centre;
16% – edge-of-centre;
42% – out-of-centre

4.11   Since 1985, Sainsbury has closed eight stores in market towns, including Bridgwater, Bury St Edmunds, Chichester, Chippenham, East Grinstead, Haverhill, Horsham and Northwich. In all cases, these were because of the opening of large replacement stores. In the case of four of these store closures, the units were either assigned to other retailers (mixture of food and non-food operators), or sub-divided into smaller retail units.

4.12   In terms of new store development and/or extensions to existing stores, at the time of the survey, Sainsburys, was actively pursuing 12 opportunities in market towns; four in town centres; seven in edge-of-centre locations; and one in an out-of-centre location. Aside from an out-of-

centre store in Stroud, and an edge-of-centre proposal in Shaftesbury, all the proposed new stores have a net sales area of 1,393 m². This is significantly smaller than the superstore benchmark, and reflects the increasingly differentiated approach being adopted by some of the main food retailers to store sizes and formats.

4.13   Since 1985, Sainsbury has closed 28 stores in district centres. A large proportion of these stores were closed because they were considered too dated and small to remain profitable. In general, these were assigned to discount food operators including Kwik Save and Robert Greig.

4.14   In terms of store openings, at the time of the survey Sainsbury was only pursuing four new store opportunities in district centres; Emersons Green (Bristol), Newton Breda (Belfast), Loughton, and Winnersh (Reading).

4.15   Somerfield operates a total of approximately 600 stores in the UK, which the company categorises as:-

41%   local high street;
28% – major high street;
19% – neighbourhood centre;
12% – edge/out-of-town.

4.16   Whilst the company does not have detailed data of store closures, Somerfield has informed us that it has closed a large number of stores since the mid 1980's; in 1986 it operated over 1,100 stores compared to the current total of around 600.

4.17   Whilst there are no specific details of the number of new stores/extensions currently being pursued, Somerfield is embarking upon an acquisitions programme and is seeking sites throughout the UK. Town centre sites able to accommodate around 2,787 m² gross are preferred. (We should point out that our retailer survey was undertaken prior to Somerfield merging with Kwik Save.)

Impact of Large Foodstores on Market Towns and District Centres

4.18   Retailers were asked to identify the number of existing stores in market towns and district centres which have witnessed an impact from any new edge/out-of-centre foodstores since 1985, and to identify those market towns/district centres which have not experienced any direct impact from new stores.

4.19   Of the 100 stores Tesco operates in market towns, only 18 have not witnessed any new store openings within their catchment area (defined by Tesco as an eight mile radius). Of the 82 stores where openings have occurred, Tesco indicate that 85% have been impacted to some degree. Only 12 stores have not witnessed any impact, and with the exception of one store, all are relatively new stores, with half located on the edge-of-town centres and the other half out-of-centre.

4.20   Tesco indicate that impacts on existing stores are often not confined to one new store opening. For example, Tesco has identified 137 'impacts' which suggests that most of the 72 stores that have been impacted upon have been affected by more than one opening. Table 4 shows that town centre stores are generally more vulnerable to impacts than stores in other locations. However, as Tesco point out, town centre stores are generally older, and have therefore had a longer period in which to experience impacts (average opening date for town centre stores is 1981; for edge-of-centre is 1984; and out-of-centre is 1991).

4.21   Tesco point out that the level of impact experienced at Tesco stores varies significantly depending on the proximity of the competitor, its offer compared with Tesco, and the catchment characteristics. Table 5 summarises the range of impacts incurred by Tesco stores in market towns since 1985. Whilst in most cases impacts have been less than 10%, some 25% have been above that level. In particular, 11 openings have resulted in impacts of up to 25%, and nine have resulted in even higher impacts.

4.22   Tesco points out that the effect of new store openings is part of the normal trading environment in which the company operates, and would expect most stores to be able to continue to trade successfully. Tesco also indicates that when the new store will be operated by the company, existing stores will often continue to trade despite suffering large impacts (e.g. see case study details of Cirencester). Tesco has indicated that its policy of keeping smaller stores trading has been reviewed in recent years, and decisions made in the 1980s would not necessarily be repeated now. In particular, fewer stores would now be closed and consideration would be given to converting a small town centre store to the Metro format. According to Tesco, this is illustrated by the Metro openings in Newbury and Andover; the latter in a former Tesco unit.

Table 4   Number of Impacts Affecting Tesco Stores in Market Towns

Town Location	Number of Impacts				
	0	1	2	3	4+
Town Centre	1	3	3	2	4
Edge-of-Centre	8	6	7	5	1
District Centre	1	0	0	0	1
Out-of-Centre	20	21	12	4	1
Total (100)	**30**	**30**	**22**	**11**	**7**

Source: Tesco Research (1996)

Table 5 **Level of Impact Experienced in Market Towns**		
Impact Level	**No. of Impacts Measured**	**Impacts Measured**
Low (0-4.99%)	40	29%
Medium (5-9.99%)	62	45%
High (10-14.99%)	15	11%
Very High (15% or more)	20	15%
TOTAL	**137**	**100%**
Source: Tesco Research (1996)		

4.23   In terms of Tesco's response to impact suffered from a competing store, the company has indicated that this '*may result in an increase in investment in the short term, with plans for a re-fit, extension or improvement of services being implemented. However, although competitor activity may result in such plans being brought forward or modified in a minor way, the decision to invest in the store would have already been made as part of our normal business plans.*' (Tesco, 1996)

Retail and Transport Impact Assessments

4.24   Retailers were asked to provide their views on when retail and transport impact assessments should be undertaken, and how current approaches can be improved in order to achieve a greater degree of consistency.

4.25   In Tesco's experience, in every instance the company is required to submit retail impact assessments in support of new foodstore proposals in out-of-centre locations. In the case of edge-of-centre proposals, such an assessment is not always required. However, where there is some debate as to whether a site is edge-of-centre or out-of-centre, retail impact assessments are usually required. Tesco indicates that this is particularly true of small market towns where the development of even a relatively small new store can represent a significant increase in total retail floorspace in the town.

4.26   Where sites are fully within town centres, Tesco indicates that retail impact assessments are only required in exceptional circumstances (e.g. where there are a number of proposals in the area and the cumulative impact is an issue). Tesco's experience suggests that the decision as to whether or not to carry out a retail impact assessment is 'determined largely by the local planning authority, rather than by the location of the proposals or any other feature'.

4.27   In terms of transportation issues, Tesco indicates that since the publication of PPG13 in March 1994, local planning authorities increasingly require assessments of the accessibility of sites by a variety of means of transport. These studies can lead to requirements for improved public transport services, and in this respect, Tesco currently operates 424 bus services at 95 sites.

4.28   Whilst assessments of the effect on car usage and trip lengths are usually required for out-of-centre sites and sometimes for edge-of-centre locations, Tesco submits such assessments, even if not requested to do so by the local planning authority, in small towns where the company considers the development of a new foodstore in whatever location would significantly reduce car borne trips for bulk food shopping in large stores in nearby centres.

4.29   Tesco employs several firms of planning and highways consultants to advise on its store development programme. Tesco supports a simple 'step by step' or 'traditional' approach to retail impact assessments. Tesco considers that this type of approach is easy to follow, and has advantages over complex mathematical models requiring computer assistance. Tesco stress the importance of the reliability of data inputs and assumptions made, and favour the use of household interview surveys to provide assistance in identifying shopping patterns and the levels of turnover in the catchment area.

4.30   Tesco consider that the calculation of percentage impact is but one step towards understanding the likely impact of a new proposal on the vitality and viability of a centre. The company reiterates some of the findings in a report they commissioned from Healey and Baker in 1995, which concluded that some of the vitality and viability indicators set out in PPG6 (1993 edition) were difficult to assess with confidence. It recommended that factors which could be most readily analysed were the functions of the centre, vacancy levels, and retailers' requirements.

4.31   Tesco considers that whilst the planning system does not at present provide a satisfactory basis for assessing the effects of large foodstores, the essential framework is in place. However, the retailer has specific concerns about the availability of data; whilst population, expenditure and growth rates are readily available, there are a number of specific deficiencies in the availability of accurate retail floorspace information, household surveys and information on retail turnover. Tesco points out that as a retailer which is frequently in contact with the planning system at both local and national levels, the company is often asked to provide information which it considers should properly have been assembled by the local authority in preparing its Local Plan or UDP.

4.32   Somerfield considers that retail assessments should be routinely required for any foodstore proposal (including store extensions) involving over 500 m² of additional sales floorspace, in edge and out-of-centre locations. The company emphasises that consistency of approach is required as smaller stores can represent the threat of a major impact where they are proposed near to smaller towns, district and local centres. Somerfield also considers that in the following circumstances a

retail impact assessment should also be required for town centre proposals where the store:-

- is over 500 m² net sales area; and

- has a sales area equivalent to or larger than 20% of existing convenience goods floorspace in the centre.

4.33   In terms of studies considering traffic generation and travel demand implications of proposals in edge and out-of-centre locations, Somerfield recommends that such studies should be submitted for schemes of 2,000 m² or above. The company considers that it would be difficult to distinguish the effects of smaller proposals from other 'background noise'.

4.34   Somerfield broadly concurs with Tesco's methodology for undertaking retail impact assessments, and suggests that the optimum approach is a 'step by step' analysis, explaining the various assumptions used and their implications. Somerfield also advocates the use of household survey data to establish existing shopping patterns, and provide a basis from which to calculate the amount of expenditure available to support existing and new floorspace.

4.35   As net margins in the food industry are low and fixed costs are high, Somerfield considers that relatively low levels of impact (e.g. 5%) can have serious implications for the viability of smaller stores in particular. Even relatively small impacts can give rise to cost-cutting responses (labour, property maintenance, etc) which all have adverse implications for the vitality and viability of centres. This point has been raised in our discussions with other retailers, both nationals and independents. Somerfield also considers that assessments need to include a thorough health check of centres likely to be affected, and in particular, the indicators in Figure 1 of PPG6 should be considered on a time-series basis.

4.36   Somerfield agrees broadly that the availability of population, expenditure and growth rates is not a problem. The principal data deficiencies relate to floorspace statistics, survey data on existing shopping patterns (e.g. a national household survey), and data on the turnover and performance of centres. Somerfield considers that the availability of these data sources would remove a large area of 'guesstimation' from retail impact assessments.

4.37   Somerfield does not consider that the planning system currently provides a satisfactory basis for assessing the scope for, and impact of new large foodstores in market towns and district centres, for the following reasons:-

- retail impact assessments involve too many subjective judgements (particularly those for which no household survey is undertaken to establish current shopping patterns);

- the system is failing to be adequately 'plan-led', partly because there remains a conflict between the general presumption in favour of the developer (e.g. PPG1) and the implied removal of that presumption for many retail proposals outside town centres as contained in the revised PPG6 (June 1996); and

- there is a lack of understanding of the economics of food retailing within the planning profession. In particular, the lack of recognition of the need of retailers to secure real annual growth in turnover and profitability to remain viable. Somerfield considers that there are limitations to the extent to which individual retailers and local authorities can improve the situation. The root cause of the problems can only be addressed at central Government level.

Summary

4.38   At the time of the survey (February 1996), Tesco was pursuing new store opportunities in 35 market towns; 22 in out-of-centre locations, and 13 in edge-of-centre locations; Similarly, Sainsbury was pursuing 12 opportunities in market towns;

four in town centre locations and seven in out-of-centre locations. The company was actively pursuing new store opportunities in four district centres.

4.39   Of the 100 market towns in which Tesco is represented, 82 have witnessed new store openings since 1985. 85% of these stores have been impacted to some degree, ranging from 3 to 40 per cent. Impact is not necessarily confined to one store opening; Tesco has measured 137 'impacts', indicating that a large proportion of their stores have witnessed cumulative impacts over a number of years.

4.40   While Tesco considers impact is an inevitable consequence of competition, and expects most of its stores to continue to trade successfully, Somerfield has highlighted that low levels of impact (e.g. 5%) can have serious consequences in terms of the viability of smaller stores in particular; this distinction is illustrated by the different store development programmes and experience of closures of the two retailers.

4.41   There appears to be some degree of consensus between retailers about the basic methodology for retail impact assessments. Retailers generally advocate a step by step approach, and endorse the use of household survey material to identify current shopping patterns. However, retailers highlight the lack of consistent and reliable data on floorspace, retail turnover and shopping patterns.

CHAPTER 5
Classification of Market Towns

Classification Criteria

5.1   This section considers the common characteristics of market towns and district centres by means of comparable data sets, and identifies characteristics which denote different sizes of market towns. To assist us in compiling a comprehensive classification, we have had regard to four key variables:-

- The number of non-food multiple retailers in each town, using Hillier Parker's *Shopping Centres of Great Britain*, 1996 Update;

- Urban area population figures from Focus;

- Goad floorspace figures (total retail floorspace and convenience floorspace); and

- Number and overall size of large food stores over 1,393 m² net (15,000 ft²).

5.2   In the absence of any up to date Census of Distribution, we explored the use of credit card data as a fifth variable, which provides a breakdown of shopping centres catchment areas, and changes over time since 1984. This may be a valuable data source for defining survey areas for detailed case studies. However, on detailed examination, we have concluded that it has limited utility in terms of the classification of towns. The data set defines catchment areas, but not market penetration levels within the defined catchment areas. Therefore, the results suggest disproportionately high catchments for small centres within densely populated areas.

5.3   Until recently, the only nationally available catchment area survey was the Pinpoint analysis, undertaken in 1989, which is considered to be outdated and of relatively limited value for the purposes of the current classification. More recently, Hillier Parker has completed and published separately a national survey of comparison shopping patterns. However, to date there is no widely available, comprehensive detailed database which defines the food shopping catchment population (as opposed to the catchment area). The only reliable data is to be derived from individual household interview surveys, commissioned by local authorities/retailers or developers on an 'ad hoc' basis.

5.4   Other indices, in particular, the level of multiple retailer representation in the town, provide a good indication of the relative catchments and profiles of different centres. This is because the number of multiples is in itself a guide to the relative strength of a centre and spending power of its catchment; the greater the number of multiples, the more attractive the centre is to shoppers, and potentially to other retailers.

5.5   The total floorspace figure is usually indicative of the importance of a centre in terms of its retail offer, although there is no fully accurate national floorspace database. Goad produce a comprehensive database, but the figures are calculated from the Goad Plan, which does not provide an accurate net or gross figure. Despite this limitation, Goad figures are useful as a means of comparison with other centres, as they are measured on the same basis, and these represent an appropriate measure for the purposes of our classification.

5.6   As part of our research to identify a comprehensive classification, we investigated the potential benefits of using the multiple count and Goad floorspace figures to calculate an index by dividing the total floorspace by the number of multiples. In general, the lower the index the greater the ratio of multiple retailers to total floorspace, and therefore the 'stronger' the centre in retailing terms. Purpose built centres, like Meadowhall, will display much lower ratios of floorspace per multiple. In contrast, declining centres may retain a large retail stock, but relatively fewer multiples (although the important contribution that independent retailers make to the character strength of market towns should not be underestimated).

5.7　We have explored a range of other indicators in order to identify whether any single index, or range of indices, produces a practical classification. The level of convenience retailing in a centre, both in absolute terms, and as a proportion of total floorspace, provides a useful indication of that centre's reliance on food retailing. This is recognised as a common characteristic of market towns and district centres, but not necessarily of the position of the centre in the hierarchy.

5.8　We have encountered problems in defining a single classification on this basis alone. The size of food superstores is such that the ranking of centres varies enormously depending on whether the centre contains a superstore, and whether superstores are within, or on the edge of the centre in question. Baldock, in Hertfordshire, graphically illustrates this point, where a large Tesco superstore serving a wide catchment suggests a disproportionately significant status for the town, which apart from Tesco contains a limited convenience and comparison retail offer.

The Classification

5.9　Having explored all the key variables, either singly or combined, we have reached the conclusion that for the purpose of devising a classification of market towns, the most appropriate and readily comprehensible determinant of the retail role and catchment of a centre is the single variable of the multiple count.

5.10　Whilst it is possible to create 'bands' of different size market towns according to their multiple count, we consider that it would be inappropriate to attempt to identify more than two bands. To do so would necessitate making arbitrary assumptions about the size and function of market towns which, by their nature, differ widely. This would undermine the credibility of the classification. Whilst the precise split between small/medium and large market towns is to some extent subjective, we set out below what we consider to be a credible two band classification, as follows:-

- 1-11 (small market towns);
- 12-25 (medium/large market towns).

5.11　The Hillier Parker Shopping Centre Classification not only provides a useful benchmark for assessing the size of market towns, it also enables an analysis of how these towns have performed over a period of time in terms of the change in the level of multiple representation. This is especially pertinent given the need to identify those market towns which are potentially most vulnerable (i.e. those which have witnessed a decline in multiple retailer representation).

5.12　The small towns category is considered to provide a realistic sample base of comparable small market towns, a number of which typically accommodate no more than one large food store. The second band, comprising centres of between 12-25 multiples generally comprises larger centres, serving more extensive catchments, where the role of large food stores is well established. This band includes towns such as Market Harborough, Saffron Walden, Petersfield and Sevenoaks. The classification excludes the largest market towns, such as Bury St Edmunds and Taunton, which have grown to serve a sub-regional retail function.

5.13　The second category of centres tends to have a wider and more long established provision of town centre and out-of-centre food superstore provision; the centres generally perform a more extensive comparison retail offer. In many cases, these towns have accommodated supermarkets in the 1980's, and have subsequently seen out-of-centre development of one or more stores.

Rams Walk Shopping Centre, Petersfield, Hampshire.

Examples of key market towns within this category include Huntingdon, Stamford, Buxton, Cirencester, Beverley, Hitchin and Bridgwater. Unlike the small, and certain medium sized market towns, the pattern of out-of-centres is now generally quite mature.

5.14 Detailed assessment of the net change in multiple retailers and their location during the last three to five years provides an important indication of relative decline/improvement in market towns and district centres. Recent assessments of centres including Dorking and Petersfield have highlighted the benefit of this analysis. In Dorking, the number of multiple retailer closures since 1994 has significantly outweighed new multiple openings; as a consequence there has been an increase in the number of service uses and charity shops in the town centre. This contrasts with the situation in Petersfield where the town centre has witnessed a marked improvement in he number of multiple retailers, partly as a consequence of lettings at the Rams Walk Shopping Centre.

5.15 In addition to analysing the number and relative change in multiple retailers, an important indication of the potential vulnerability of market towns and district centres is the basis of lettings for all new town centre stores. In particular, an increasing trend towards short term/five year leases, could be symptomatic of a decline in retailer confidence in the town, and therefore genuine cause for concern.

Criteria for Selection of Case Studies

5.16   The two band classification has been used to draw up a sample for detailed case studies. These are an integral part of our research, and test some of the general conclusions drawn from the literature review, and the local authority and retailer surveys.

5.17   It is not possible to achieve a fully representative sample of case studies from which to draw general conclusions about the effects of large foodstore development on different market towns and district centres. For this reason, the case studies should be considered as providing an illustration of the range of consequences that can occur, as a means of drawing parallels with similar situations arising in the future.

5.18   It was agreed with the Steering Group that the case studies were to be selected to ensure an appropriate spread of small and medium-sized

market towns and district centres, and to identify and differentiate between the effects of large foodstores in edge-of-centre and out-of-centre locations. This enables us to test two hypotheses; first, that smaller centres tend to be more sensitive to the effect of large out-of-centre foodstores, and second, that out-of-centre stores have different effects to in or edge-of-centre stores.

5.19   Whilst it would be desirable to achieve a broad geographical spread of market towns and district centres, we do not consider this is essential. Our priority has been to identify as broad a range of market town and district centre scenarios as possible, and whilst there may be some regional differences, we do not consider that these are likely to have significant implications or in any way undermine the conclusions of the study.

5.20   We have focused on what we consider to be typical small and medium-sized market towns, where foodstore development has taken place during the last five years. This enables us to

---

Table 6 Case Study Market Towns and District Centres

Stage 1

	Edge-of-Centre	Out-of-Centre
Small	Warminster (8)	Fakenham (8)
Medium/Large	Cirencester (19) (Pilot Survey)	St Neots (13) *Northfield (12)

Stage 2

	Edge-of-Centre	Out-of-Centre
Small	–	Ashby-de-la-Zouch (7) Leominster (5)
Medium/Large	–	* Ferndown (4) * Portchester (2)

Notes 1:   Small denotes multiple count of 1-11
            Medium/Large denotes multiple count of 12-25

2:    * denotes district centres

3:    Figure in brackets denotes number of multiples according to Hillier Parker's Shopping Centres Classification

consider 'before and after' effects, and to make informed judgements as to those centres where the effects may not yet have fully manifested themselves.

5.21   We have also attempted as far as possible to include a broadly representative sample of different foodstore operators. We have also, where possible, chosen case study towns/centres where consultants have previously undertaken work, so that we could assess the robustness of their approach, particularly in respect of assessing the likely impact of the new foodstore.

5.22   To ensure a robust and consistent methodology is employed for all case studies, it was agreed with the Steering Group to undertake a pilot survey. The agreed methodology was subsequently employed in the remaining eight case studies.

5.23   The eight case studies were divided into two tranches comprising four case studies in each (five market towns and three district centres). This allowed further fine-tuning of the methodology and approach, if necessary, and it enabled us to review the selection of case studies for the second stage to alter the mix of market towns/district

centres, and edge-of-centre/out-of-centre stores to ensure that as far as possible we covered the full range of potential issues.

5.24   The selection of a 'typical' district centre was problematical. District centres are, by their nature, difficult to define and display a wider range of characteristics than market towns. It was agreed therefore that in the second tranche of case studies, we would include two district centres to cover, as far as possible, the particular problems facing district centres.

5.25   Having regard to these criteria, Table 6 identifies the market towns and district centres selected for detailed case studies. The results of the case studies are described in the next chapter.

CHAPTER 6
The Market Town Case Studies

6.1   Case studies were undertaken in six market towns; Cirencester; Warminster; Ashby-de-la-Zouch; Fakenham; St Neots; and Leominster.

6.2   Each market town case study was based on a specially commissioned household interview survey of the centre's catchment using a questionnaire developed from the pilot survey and agreed by the Steering Group. The survey identified current shopping patterns as well as those prior to the opening of the edge-of-centre/out-of-centre foodstores.

6.3   The surveys were undertaken on a postcode sector basis, and in each sector or grouping of sectors, 50 interviews were carried out. The sample interviews were derived from a random selection across all the phone numbers in each postcode sector or combination of sectors. The total sample of the catchment areas were therefore a random sample of households stratified to give a pre-determined sample in each sector.

6.4   Examples of the issues covered by the survey included:-

- where shoppers do most of their food shopping;

- frequency of visits to the store/centre;

- proportion of total weekly food spend accounted for by the store/centre;

- mode of transport;

- other stores/centres shoppers visit for food shopping;

- whether shoppers undertake combined shopping trips;

- whether the frequency of the foodstore visits has changed as a result of the new foodstore;

- where shoppers used to go for most of their food shopping requirements before the store opened; and

- whether the development of the new store has affected the destination, and frequency of visits for non-food shopping.

6.5   The survey was designed to identify changes in what we consider to be the most relevant variables in identifying the tangible and directly attributable effects of large foodstores on market towns and district centres. The key variables applied to each of the case studies are set out in Figure 1.

6.6   For each of the case study market towns a summary table of Assessment Criteria is included in the Appendices.

6.7   In addition to the household survey, we undertook discussions with the local planning authorities, Chambers of Commerce and key retailers in each of the case study towns to gauge the actual levels of trade diversion and any practical consequences such as job losses and reduced investment levels. We also undertook an overall analysis of the level and quality of food shopping provision in each town before and after the development of the new stores, and the accessibility of all shopping facilities to all sectors in the catchment.

6.8   'Quality' has been assessed having regard to the range and choice of food shopping facilities. We have considered convenience in terms of accessibility, product lines and other features (pharmacy, post office, dry cleaning, etc).

Figure 1 Assessment Criteria

Criteria	Explanation
Catchment area profile	To what extent has the new store altered the catchment profile of the town. For example, has it increased clawback of expenditure?
Shopping patterns	Changes in the destination and frequency of food and non-food shopping?
Quantitative Impact	Before and after market shares, and trade diversion from the town centre.
Employment Impact	Changes in the level and type of employment.
Modal split/Public Transport	Modal split to stores in the area and any changes due to the new store
Car ownership/availability	Level of car ownership within the primary catchment area. Whether a car is normally available for the main food shop. This will have an influence on the mode used for food shopping
Car-parking	Provision, pricing and level of use of car-parks in the town and whether there has been any perceptible change as a result of the new store
Linked Trips/Store Location	Do people combine food shopping with other activities on the same trip, particularly within the town centre. Has the occurrence of linked trips been affected by the move to the new store?
Travel distance	Has there been any material change in vehicle mileage as a result of the new store?

6.9   Whilst we have endeavoured to identify changes in employment in the retail sector in each of the case study towns, the paucity of comprehensive information at a 'local' level has precluded any detailed analysis. We consider the issue of impact on employment in the retail sector from a wider perspective in Chapter Eight.

6.10   In the case of edge-of-centre stores, we have analysed the effectiveness of linkages between the new store and the town centre. We have also considered the distance between the store and the main shopping area, the attractiveness of links, and extent to which they are facilitating 'linked shopping trips'.

6.11   Having analysed the extent of any change in the variables set out in Figure 1, we have analysed the extent to which these changes have affected the economic health of each market town, as measured against the relevant indicators set out in PPG6. These include:-

- diversity of uses;

- retailer representation and intentions to change representation;

- shopping rents;

- proportion of vacant street level property;

- commercial yields;

- pedestrian flows;

- accessibility;

- customer views and behaviour;

- perception of safety and occurrence of crime; and

- state of the town centre environmental quality.

Summary of Results

CIRENCESTER

6.12   Since 1994, Cirencester has witnessed the development of 2 new superstores; a large out-of-centre Tesco in February 1994, and a smaller edge-of-centre Waitrose in November 1995. Whilst the primary purpose of the pilot survey was to assess the impact of the edge-of-centre Waitrose on Cirencester town centre, we have also had regard to the effects of the out-of-centre Tesco.

6.13   Cirencester is an attractive historic market town with an urban area population of 15,217. The town is located on the A417/A433, and is approximately 16 miles south of Cheltenham; 19 miles south-east of Gloucester; and 17 miles north of Swindon. The town has an above average proportion of people employed in transport and communication industries, distribution, hotels and catering; the latter of which reflects its important tourism function. Primary industries (farming, fishing and forestry) also account for a higher than average proportion of the workforce. Agriculture continues to be an important feature of Cirencester; evidenced by the livestock market in the town.

6.14   According to the CCN Lifestyle groupings, Cirencester is a relatively affluent centre with a significantly higher proportion of high income families compared to the national average (20.4% compared with 9.9%). Unemployment in Cirencester is currently 4.8% compared with a national average of approximately 7.8%.

6.15   Cirencester has approximately 51,330 m^2 of gross town centre floorspace, comprising 267 street level units. According to Hillier Parker's *Shopping Centres of Great Britain Classification*, Cirencester

Cirencester town centre, looking towards Market Place.

has a multiple count of 19, including W H Smith, Boots, Woolworths, Burtons, Halfords and Superdrug. In addition, the town centre has an attractive mix of independent comparison retailers selling a range of antiques and crafts.

6.16   The town is relatively well served by a range of independent and multiple convenience retailers, and has a twice weekly open market, which sells a range of fresh food and non-food items. The provision of main foodstores, which collectively represent the majority of total convenience floorspace serving Cirencester, is shown in Table 7 below.

6.17   Both Tesco stores are relatively modern, and provide a full range of convenience goods. The out-of-centre Tesco is the largest foodstore serving Cirencester, and provides a coffee shop, petrol filling station and in-store pharmacy. The new Waitrose offers a comparable quality of shopping environment, and also includes a coffee shop. However, this store is smaller than Tesco and does not have a petrol filling station or pharmacy. The

Table 7	**Main Foodstore Provision – Cirencester**		
Store	**Location**	**Size (sq m net)**	**Opening Date**
Tesco	Farrell Close (town centre)	2,393	March 1981
Iceland	Dyer Street (town centre)	1,115	–
Tesco	Kingsmeadow (out-of-centre)	3,695	February 1994
Somerfield	Love Lane (out-of-centre)	1,858	June 1975
Waitrose	Hammond Way (edge-of-centre)	2,358	November 1995

Source: Hillier Parker, IGD, Retailer Figures

Cirencester edge-of-centre Waitrose, (in centre distance).

Somerfield store is relatively dated in appearance and in qualitative terms generally offers a less comprehensive provision than its competitors.

6.18   In terms of the changes, the out-of-centre Tesco had a significant impact on trade diversion from food and non-food town centre retailers, including the town centre Tesco. The store now dominates food retailing in Cirencester; it achieves the highest market share and serves an almost exclusively car borne retail function, particularly since the bus services which initially served the store have been diverted.

6.19   The Waitrose opened in November 1995 on the edge of the town centre, just within the 300m guideline identified in PPG6. However, the lack of functional linkages and the relatively low level of walk-in trade to the store suggest that it does not, in practice, perform the role of an edge-of-centre store. The implications of this in terms of the use of distance as a criterion for defining adequately edge-of-centre stores are considered in Chapter 10.

6.20   The most direct impact of the edge-of-centre Waitrose was the closure of the town centre Waitrose on Dyer Street; the additional cumulative impact on other retailers in the town centre appears to have been less significant overall. Some retailers experienced an improvement in sales, while others saw a significant drop in turnover. Based on our research, the impact of Waitrose appears to have been broadly negative rather than positive.

6.21   Our analysis suggests that the edge-of-centre Waitrose has not clawed back significant convenience goods trade from competing centres, or from the out-of-centre Tesco. The store does not appear to have extended Cirencester's catchment beyond that already secured by the larger and more accessible (by car) out-of-centre Tesco; nor has the store diverted any significant proportion of trade from the out-of-centre Tesco back into the centre. There is no evidence of any additional spin-off non-food trade being secured as a consequence of the new Waitrose.

6.22   In terms of the modal split and the propensity for linked trips, while the Tesco serves an almost exclusively car borne trade, with relatively few linked trips, the town centre Tesco secures by far the highest proportion of public transport and walk-in trade, and the highest proportion of combined shopping trips. The edge-of-centre Waitrose secures a materially higher proportion of linked trips than the out-of-centre Tesco, but still serves a largely car borne catchment, and overall may have caused a shift in modal split towards the use of the car.

6.23   Whilst we have been unable to draw any substantive conclusions regarding the effects of either proposal on the overall level or character of employment, or the wider local economy, it is likely that in totality employment in retailing in the town has increased as a result of the new foodstores. In particular, Cirencester has a low and falling level of unemployment, and has not witnessed a decline in the number of shop units in the town centre in contrast to national trends.

6.24   Overall, following the decentralisation of food shopping to Tesco, we consider that the Waitrose has further reinforced the pattern of decentralisation of convenience shopping in Cirencester; and in this respect has reinforced the change in shopping patterns caused by the Tesco. However, leaving aside more significant localised effects resulting from the closure of the town centre Waitrose, the cumulative impact of the edge-of-centre Waitrose has been much less significant.

6.25   Despite significant changes in shopping patterns and levels of trade diversion, and the loss of a principal town centre foodstore, on the basis of all the relevant indicators in PPG6, the vitality and viability of Cirencester town centre does not appear to have been undermined by either store.

6.26   The only indications of any deterioration in the vitality and viability of the town centre are retail yields, and the apparent decline in the support for the market. These may be accounted for by short term factors, including the vacant Waitrose store (now occupied by Argos). Alternatively, the full implications of the new stores may have not necessarily been experienced to date.

FAKENHAM

6.27   The purpose of this case study was to assess the impact of the opening of Safeway on an out-of-centre site at Clipbush Road in November 1994. Fakenham is a small historic market town with an urban population of 6,456. The town is located at the junction of the A1065, A148 and A1067, approximately 25 km to the north-east of Swaffham, 37 km to the east of King's Lynn and 32 km to the south-west of Cromer.

6.28   Fakenham is characterised by an ageing population compared with the national average in all age bands from 45 years above. It is also characterised by higher than national average

representation in lower socio-economic groups and under representation in higher socio-economic groups. Despite this age profile, Fakenham has a mobile population with car ownership significantly above the national average (76.4% compared with 66.6%).

6.29   Fakenham has a significantly above average proportion of its employed work force in primary industries (14.2% compared with 3.3% nationally), which can be almost entirely attributed to people working within the agricultural sector (14.1%), reflecting the continued importance of farming in the area. Manufacturing employment mirrors the national average which can be largely attributed to the presence of the Fakenham Industrial Estate

Fakenham town centre.

outside the town centre where there are a range of light engineering companies, many of which are allied to the agricultural sector.

6.30   The trend in employment in Fakenham broadly follows the national average (7.1% in April 1996 compared with the then national average of 7.8%). Fakenham has approximately 30,955 m² of gross town centre floorspace comprising 119 units. According to Hillier Parker's *Shopping Centres of Great Britain Classification*, Fakenham has a multiple count of eight, including; Boots, Currys, Woolworths, and Freeman Hardy Willis.

6.31   The largest retailer in the town is W J Aldiss which operates from a traditional town centre department store on three storeys at Upper Market and a modern retail warehouse located off Old Lane to the south east of the town centre, opposite the car park from Budgens. This store in particular is a major magnet for the town but does not appear to have mitigated the loss of convenience trade. Other attractions include the Charter Market which operates from The Square on Thursdays. There are a limited number of specialist comparison goods retailers including antiques stores, but generally the comparison shopping offer of the town is relatively poor.

6.32   The provision of main foodstores in and outside of Fakenham is shown in Table 8.

6.33   Budgens is the only foodstore of any size left in the town centre following the closure of Lo Cost in March 1995. This store only has a net floorspace of 1,003 m² and is linked to a modern shopping arcade known as Millers Walk. Following the closure of the Post Office on Holt Road, Budgens now also includes a Post Office counter. The Lo-Cost unit which traded briefly as Spar before its closure has remained vacant ever since.

6.34   Rainbow was the first out-of-centre foodstore to be developed in the Fakenham area and opened in 1983. It is located on Holt Road less than one km from the town centre but provides a relatively poor quality shopping environment. It is largely housed in the former Dalgety Spillers premises, comprising two storey corrugated sheeting clad sheds. It has a poor range of in-store facilities with car parking split between the front and rear of the store.

6.35   In contrast, the Safeway store at Clipbush Lane which opened in 1994 provides a high quality shopping environment in a readily accessible location at the junction of the two principal roads into Fakenham, the A148 and A1067. It has a full range of facilities including a delicatessen, bakery, large coffee shop, newsagent and a separate petrol filling station with associated kiosk and car wash.

6.36   The impact study supporting the Safeway application concluded that the Lo-Cost would have a residual turnover per ft² above the operator's national average. The Argyll Group stated its intentions to continue trading from the Lo-Cost after the opening of Safeway. In practice, soon after the opening of Safeway in November 1994, the Lo-Cost store

Table 8 **Main Foodstore Provision – Fakenham**			
Store	Location	Size (sq m net)	Opening Date
Budgens	Millers Walk (town centre)	1,003	October 1988
Lo-Cost	Norwich Street (town centre)	272	Closed March 1995
Rainbow (Anglia Regional Co-op)	Holt Road (out-of-centre) Convenience foodstore Home & Garden	1,732 348	June 1983
Safeway	Clipbush Road (out-of-centre)	2,322	November 1994
Source: Hillier Parker, IGD, Retailer Figures, North Norfolk DC			

(operated by Argyll, also the parent company of Safeway) closed and re-opened as Spar which closed soon after in early 1995.

6.37   Our survey points to the percentage of people using Fakenham town centre for their main food shopping decreasing from 14% to 5%, an impact of 64%. Levels of impact appear high due to the relatively small initial market shares. Therefore, the practical implications of these levels of impact might not be as high as the figures suggest. Anglia Regional Co-operative Society's figures show a 36% impact on the Rainbow store following the opening of Safeway, which subsequently increased to 38%, indicating an ongoing impact.

6.38   We also obtained annual turnover figures from selection of anonymous comparison retailers which showed two patterns. First, the turnover of all six retailers fell between 1992 to 1994 before the opening of Safeway by an average of 12.3%. Second, following the opening of Safeway with one exception the turnover of all the retailers fell, ranging between 0.1% and 24.6%. This appears to substantiate the views of local traders and the Chamber of Trade and Commerce that the period from when the Safeway application was determined by the District Council to its opening was marked by uncertainty and a lack of business confidence reflected in declining turnovers. While this cannot wholly be attributed to the anticipated opening of Safeway, given the retail recession occurring at that time, it is likely to have been a factor in retailers' decision whether to continue trading in the town.

6.39   The Safeway store is not surrounded by a residential catchment, has a poor bus service, and tends to be visited less frequently than the other stores. Therefore, not surprisingly, it is almost exclusively served by car. Conversely the Budgens in the town centre is within walking distance of residential areas and is used more for small purchases. These factors are reflected in the walk-in trade of 30%. The Budgens is also close to the main bus terminus at Market Place, and therefore is accessible from a number of areas by bus. The Rainbow store falls between the Safeway and the Budgens in a locational sense and its modal split reflects this. The overall modal split for customers visiting all stores has not changed as a result of the opening of Safeway.

6.40   There is a significantly greater linking of trips from the town centre Budgens compared with Rainbow and Safeway (70% compared with 45% and 53% respectively), although the level of linkage for the two out-of-centre stores is still fairly high.

6.41   Overall, there has been a slight reduction in distance travelled to the transfer of customers from stores further away, e.g. King's Lynn. However, these form a relatively small proportion of Safeway's customers. The majority of transfers occurred from stores within Fakenham, where the distance travelled is likely to be similar. This distance saving will be offset by the change in modal shift, a small increase in frequency of visits and decrease in linking of trips. Therefore any decrease in total travel distance is likely to be small and of little significance.

6.42   The deteriorating trading conditions within the town centre have led to falling rents, resulting in reduced investment in the town centre. The flexibility shown by some landlords in the town may be suppressing the 'real' level of vacancies which would otherwise exist if rental holidays were not offered. Furthermore, some units are for sale in the town but are not on the open market, and therefore the visual evidence of vacancies within the town may not reflect the actual position.

ST NEOTS

6.43   The purpose of this case study was to assess the impact of the opening of the out-of-centre Tesco at Barford Road, Eynesbury in June 1995 on St Neots town centre.

6.44   St Neots is a large historic market town with an urban area population of 13,470 within a wider built-up area including Eaton Ford, Eaton Socon and Eynesbury with a resident population of 25,116. The town is readily accessible to the A1 and A428 and is approximately 20 km north-east of Bedford and 29 km west of Cambridge.

6.45   A particular feature of the town is the importance of manufacturing employment reflecting its development as a post-war overspill town for London. It has a below average proportion of high income families (3.7%

St Neots town centre.

compared with 9.9%), but unemployment has remained consistently below the national average.

6.46   St Neots has approximately 40,366 m^2 of gross town centre floorspace comprising 190 street level retail units. According to Hillier Parker's *Shopping Centres of Great Britain Classification*, St Neots has a multiple count of 13 including Woolworths, Dorothy Perkins, Burtons, Superdrug and Boots. Unusually for a town of its size, St Neots has two department stores: the Westgate Co-op and Barretts of St Neots. These, together with other large independent retail businesses such as Brittains furnishers provide St Neots with particular attractions which other similar sized market towns do not have. All the stores are located on the High Street which provides St Neots with a strong focus for comparison retailing.

6.47   The town also caters for smaller more specialist retail businesses in small unit shop development such as The Cross Keys Shopping Centre, and Church Walk. This is complemented by the market which operates on Thursdays. St Neots has one of the largest market squares in England, and thus provides a significant attraction accommodating a wide range of stallholders.

6.48   The town centre contains two attractive, relatively modern food supermarkets, Waitrose and Somerfield, but following the closure of Dewhurst, and excluding confectioners, tobacconists and newsagents, the only small convenience store left in the town centre is Hamiltons at Cross Keys Mall, which sells pet supplies in addition to operating as a greengrocer.

Table 9 Main Foodstore Provision – St. Neots

Store	Location	Size (sq m net)	Opening Date
Waitrose	Priory Lane (town centre)	1,273	March 1987
Somerfield	Tebbutts Road (town centre)	1,151	March 1987
Iceland	High Street (town centre)	650	–
Tesco	Barford Road, Eynesbury (out-of-centre)	1,979	June 1995
Rainbow (Anglia Regional Co-op)	Great North Road, Eaton Ford (out-of-centre)	1,115	October 1991

Source : Hillier Parker, IGD, Retailer Figures

6.49   The Rainbow at Eaton Ford was the first out-of-centre store in St Neots and was a relocation from the town centre in the unit adjacent to the Westgate department store on the High Street. It offers a relatively limited range of goods with few customer facilities. In contrast, the Tesco at Barford Road is the largest foodstore serving St Neots and provides a coffee shop, petrol filling station and in-store pharmacy. The pharmacy is a direct transfer of the E S Calcutt business from Market Square.

6.50   Following the opening of Tesco, outflow of expenditure to other centres appears to have been reduced substantially. Although the market share of the town centre decreased from 24% to 18%, the majority of the increase in trade retention is derived from clawback of expenditure (15%). In this way, the increase in the market share of out-of-centre stores has not been at the expense of diminishing severely the town centre's market share. The catchment area of Waitrose and Somerfield has not changed markedly since the opening of Tesco.

6.51   Just over a third of Tesco shoppers previously used St Neots town centre or the Rainbow at Eaton Ford. 22% of shoppers transferred from the town centre Waitrose store with a further 9% from the town centre

Somerfield. In the town centre the pattern of frequency of visits to the main foodstores did not change significantly after the opening of Tesco.

6.52   The distribution of trade draw to Tesco reflects the two factors. First, the largest single source of trade diversion was from the largest nearest store catering for bulk food purchases – Waitrose in St Neots town centre. In contrast, the relative limitations of the Somerfield store, in terms of the range of goods sold appears to have contributed to lower trade diversion. Second, those shoppers who are already choosing to use large out-of-centre foodstores in nearby centres, particularly Huntingdon and Bedford, were willing to transfer their trade to a closer more convenient store, in the majority of cases operated by the same retailer (Tesco).

6.53   One of the main convenience retailers in St Neots is now trading at 72% of its pre-Tesco level, despite increasing trading hours by approximately 10% since the opening of that store. The Rainbow store at Eaton Ford experienced a 31% fall in turnover in the year after the opening of Tesco. In contrast, the sample of comparison goods retailers do not appear to have been affected by the opening of Tesco.

6.54 In one of the major town centre convenience retailers, we understand that the number of staff in the store was reduced to 78% following the opening of Tesco. Following an increase in trading hours, it now stands at 88% of its pre-Tesco level. However, we have not been able to obtain any reliable data on employment changes in St Neots as a whole, as a consequence of the opening of Tesco.

6.55 Overall, the opening of the out-of-centre Tesco has increased the combined town centre and out-of-centre market share, but not at the expense of a significant decline in the town centre's market share. There has been clawback of expenditure from competing stores in nearby centres, especially Bedford and Huntingdon, particularly from stores also operated by Tesco. The effect of this clawback of expenditure has been to reduce travel distances, but this has been mitigated by the reduction of linked trips within St Neots town centre. The net effect is therefore largely neutral.

6.56 The reduction in linked trips has had a negligible effect on the town's comparison retailers, and new entrants have improved the choice of comparison shopping opportunities. Having regard to the indicators in PPG6, St Neots remains a relatively vital and viable centre which does not appear to have been affected seriously by the opening of Tesco.

WARMINSTER

6.57 A new Safeway superstore opened on the edge of Warminster town centre, in June 1992. Shortly afterwards, Safeway's existing store in the Three Horseshoes Mall in the town centre closed. This unit is now occupied by a Lo-Cost foodstore. The Safeway store is within an easy walking distance of the town centre. However, the store's entrance turns its back on the town centre and is orientated towards its own surface level car park.

6.58 Warminster is an attractive historic market town with an urban population of approximately 17,000 in 1991. The town is 14 km to the south of Trowbridge town centre which provides a more comprehensive shopping offer. Salisbury is 34 km to the south. The district is over-represented, in relation to the national average, in the number of employees in primary and manufacturing industries. The level of representation in the service sector (including banking and finance) is also low in comparison to the national average.

6.59 Warminster is dominated by the presence of the Battlesbury Barracks and the School of Infantry. The levels of military personnel in these facilities has increased with the relocation of personnel from Germany.

Warminster edge-of-centre Safeway (looking towards town centre, store located immediately to left of photo).

Table 10 Main Foodstore Provision – Warminster			
Store	**Location**	**Size (m² net)**	**Opening Date**
Safeway	Weymouth Street (edge-of-centre)	2,276	June 1992
Lo-Cost	Three Horse Shoes Mall (town centre) formerly the old Safeway unit	846	Autumn 1992
Kwik Save	Market Place (town centre)	500	–
Lidl	Station Road (out-of-centre)	799	February 1995

Source: IDG, Retailer figures

6.60   The town centre includes approximately 44,000 m² of retail floorspace (gross) and the Hillier Parker Shopping Centres of Great Britain recorded that the town had eight multiple retailers. These include Boots the Chemist, Peacocks clothing, BeWise discount clothing and the Edinburgh Woollen Mill. The town has a number of independent retailers providing both comparison and convenience goods in addition to a weekly market held in the car park to the rear of the Three Horseshoes Shopping Mall.

6.61   The main foodstores in and around Warminster town centre include the Safeway store, Weymouth Street, Kwik Save, Market Place and a Lidl discount store on the edge of the town on Station Road. The Gateway store, 55-57 Market Place, closed soon after the Safeway opening in February 1994.

6.62   The new Safeway store on the edge of the town centre provides modern convenience retailing facilities including a delicatessen counter and in-house bakery. There is also an adjacent petrol filling station. The store does not have an in-store pharmacy.

6.63   The former Safeway unit in the Three Horseshoes Mall is currently occupied by Lo-Cost (part of the Safeway group). This store occupies a smaller floorspace than previously but provides a reasonable product range for its size including

freshly packaged meat, fruit and vegetables. This store is immediately adjacent to the town's principal free surface level car park.

6.64   Since the Safeway opening, the Gateway store in Warminster town centre (Market Place) has closed. This is perhaps unsurprising given the overall increase in food floorspace in Warminster with the opening of the new store. The majority of Safeway's market share (45%) has been drawn from the former Safeway in the Three Horseshoes Mall. Little trade has been drawn from other nearby modern supermarkets in the catchment area. Only 10% of trade has been drawn from stores in Trowbridge. The only other store in the immediate area providing large scale retail facilities (Normans at Crockerton) has suffered only a 4% transfer of its shoppers to the new store.

6.65   We consider that whilst the Safeway store is within a relatively easy walking distance of the town's main retail frontage, its orientation is not ideal in terms of encouraging linked trips. The importance of not only the distance of a store from the town centre, but also the functional linkages between the two, are considered in more detail in Chapter 10.

6.66   Some 42% of trips to the store are for a sole purpose (i.e. not linked with any other activity). The new store opening has not affected the frequency of visits to the town for main food shopping. The frequency of visits to the new Safeway store is virtually identical to that recorded by respondents using the former Safeway store in The Three Horseshoes Mall.

6.67   We have been unable to identify any significant changes in the indicators set out in Figure 1 of PPG6 that might indicate a change in the vitality and viability of the town centre. There has been an increase in the number of comparison goods retailers in particular those in the ladieswear, furniture and carpet sector. This has included the introduction of a number of national multiple retailers such as Peacocks and the Edinburgh Woollen Mill.

6.68   There has been a relatively large increase in the number of vacancies (from 17% in September 1990 to 24% in January 1997). This can largely be explained by the completion of the Cornhill development which provides a number of small retail units that have mostly stayed vacant since completion. The other vacancies in the town can be explained by strategic decisions made at head office level of retailers rather than responses to changed local circumstances.

6.69   As the new Safeway store has been open for almost five years, we consider that the most significant impacts would have come to light by now. On the basis of our analysis of the household survey and our assessment of the indicators in Figure 1 of PPG6, we have been unable to identify any substantive change in the vitality and viability of Warminster town centre.

6.70   Perhaps surprisingly for an edge-of-centre store, the household survey has not shown a higher level of linkage between the store and the town centre, reflecting the relatively poor physical links between the two. Therefore, the new Safeway store does not appear to have made any positive contribution to the vitality and viability of the town centre, although it has improved the range of convenience goods available to the town's shoppers.

LEOMINSTER

6.71   Safeway opened an out-of-centre superstore in August 1992. The opening of this store represents an opportunity to identify the longer term consequences of an out-of-centre foodstore for a town centre which hitherto had been dependent on a diverse range of town centre food retailers.

6.72   The store is located approximately one mile to the west of Leominster town centre on the A44, and given its strategic location on a major 'A' road, is accessible from a relatively wide area. The route between the town centre and the store is uphill, and is predominantly residential in character. Functional linkages between the store and the town centre are extremely limited.

6.73   Leominster is an attractive historic town in Hereford and Worcester with an urban area population of approximately 9,545. The town is located at the junction of the A44 and A49 and is approximately 13 miles north of Hereford; 25 miles west of Worcester; and 28 miles south-west of Kidderminster.

6.74   Leominster is the focal point for employment within the district, and has a higher than national average proportion of people employed in manufacturing; a large proportion of which are based at Leominster Industrial Estate. Agriculture continues to be an important element for local economy, evidenced by the relocation of the livestock market from the town centre to an out-of-centre site adjacent to the A49 bypass. The unemployment rate in Leominster in April 1996 was 6.4% compared with the national average of 7.8%. During the last five years, unemployment levels have been consistently below the national average.

Leominster town centre.

6.75 The town centre has a gross floorspace of approximately 34,904 m^2, comprising 211 street level retail units. According to Hillier Parker's classification of shopping centres, Leominster has five multiple retailers; significantly less than the competing higher order centres of Hereford and Worcester. A large proportion of comparison retailing is dominated by independent retailers; many of which sell specialist/niche products (antiques and crafts).

6.76 Somerfield is the principal main food retailer in the town centre, in addition to which there is a Kwik Save on the edge of the town centre which opened in November 1994, and a relatively broad range of small independent food retailers. The provision of main foodstores serving Leominster is shown in Table 11.

6.77 Safeway has widened slightly the catchment area of Leominster to the north, south and east, albeit at the expense of the town centre foodstores. In eight of the 16 postcode sectors surveyed, Safeway draws more than 20% of expenditure, with the highest being 70% (the area immediately surrounding Safeway's store). This suggests that notwithstanding the decline in retention levels in the town centre, the Safeway has met a qualitative deficiency which was not previously met by the town centre food retailers.

Table 11 Main Foodstore Provision In And Around Leominster			
Store	Location	Size (m^2 net)	Opening Date
Somerfield	Dishley Street, Leominster) (town centre)	756	1980(?)
Kwik Save	Westbury Street, Leominster (town centre)	929 (gross)	September 1994
Safeway	Barons Cross Road, Leominster (town centre)	2,322	August 1992
Somerfield	Upper Galdeford, Ludlow (town centre)	1,046	August 1987
Tesco	Bewell Street, Hereford	2,988	September 1983
Sainsbury	Barton Yard, Hereford	2,594	August 1988
Safeway	Commercial Road, Hereford	3,307	March 1990

Source: IGD, Retailer Figures

6.78   Whilst the out-of-centre Safeway has increased the combined town centre and out-of-centre convenience goods market share, this has been at the expense of a significant decline in the town centre's market share. The store now dominates food retailing in Leominster; it achieves the highest market share and serves an almost exclusively car borne retail function.

6.79   The most direct impact of the store was on the town centre Somerfield, which witnessed an impact of approximately 30%. The store continues to trade well, and underwent a refit in January 1995, and more recently in May 1997. Notwithstanding this, between June 1991 and June 1995, the number of convenience retailers in the town centre fell from 31 to 22. In particular, two centrally located supermarkets (Saverite and Lo-Cost) closed. One of these prominent units still remains vacant. In addition, a number of the smaller independent convenience retailers who continue to trade appear to have witnessed a significant decline in turnover; one reported a fall of 30% immediately following the opening of Safeway.

6.80   Discussions with non-food retailers suggest that some have witnessed a decline in their turnover since Safeway opened, although other factors including business rates revaluation in 1994 and the general economic recession were considered to be contributory factors. In particular, Boots indicated that whilst its store witnessed a nominal impact of 9%, the adjusted impact was only 1.5%, suggesting no significant long-term impact. This may, in part, be explained by the absence of an in-store pharmacy at Safeway.

6.81   24% of Safeway shoppers previously used the Somerfield in Leominster town centre, and a further 18% transferred from other foodstores in the town centre. In terms of clawback of trade, 19% of Safeway shoppers previously used large foodstores in Hereford. A further 5% of Safeway shoppers previously used foodstores in Ludlow. This suggests that the store has been relatively successful in clawing back trade from competing superstores.

6.82   In the town centre, the pattern of frequency of visits has changed slightly following Safeway's opening. In particular, a higher proportion of Somerfield shoppers now use the store on a daily basis, although a large proportion still choose to spend most of their food expenditure at the store. This suggests that whilst Somerfield has lost some of its periodic bulk shoppers, it still performs a main food shopping role. This is consistent with our own observations of trading at the store. However, in terms of other Leominster foodstores, the change in the pattern of expenditure has been more marked with significantly more shoppers now

65

spending less than 25% of their expenditure in these stores. The loss of the Saverite and Lo-Cost supermarkets are likely to have been contributory factors in explaining this shift.

6.83   In terms of modal split, a greater proportion of people who now shop at Safeway used to travel to their previous main foodstore by bus and walking, suggesting that Safeway has led to a small increase in the use of the car. Although the Safeway store has a lower proportion of linked trips compared to town centre food retailers, 63% of Safeway shoppers indicated that they usually undertake a linked trip with Leominster town centre. This compares to 52% of Safeway shoppers who previously combined trips with Leominster.

6.84   Whilst 47% of shoppers who use Safeway previously used stores outside Leominster town centre, it is likely that the distance they travel to do their main food shopping has decreased. However, only 45% of those interviewed who shop at Safeway live within the postal sectors of Leominster, and its immediately adjacent postal sectors. It is unclear therefore, whether there has been any overall increase or decrease in the distance travelled by Safeway shoppers since the store opened. We consider that the overall change is likely to be broadly neutral.

6.85   In addition to the decline in the number of convenience retailers, there has been a modest fall in the number of comparison retailers, and a shift towards more specialist type outlets, (e.g. antiques and craft shops). Service uses have increased significantly since Safeway opened, although they are currently only marginally above the national average.

6.86   Vacancy levels in the town centre rose from 16 in June 1991 to 36 in May 1997, and are significantly above the national average. These vacancies are accounted for partly by the decline in the number of convenience retailers, and also the large number of vacant units in the Buttercross Arcade (nine) which was developed at the time of the opening of Safeway.

6.87   As a direct response to the opening of Safeway, the 'Loyal To Leominster' campaign (initiated by a town centre retailer in May 1996) has been successful in raising the profile of the

town centre, and has contributed to an improvement in the turnover of at least some participating retailers. In addition, the District Council, having been assisted by the Town Regeneration Forum, was awarded approximately £2.2 million of Single Regeneration Budget (SRB) funding to help improve the environment of the town centre.

6.88   It would appear that the opening of Safeway has had a detrimental effect on the vitality and viability of Leominster town centre, and has led to a significant decentralisation of the town's convenience goods provision. Nonetheless, the general decline is also a function of other factors, including the economic recession and the business rates revaluation. The response from town centre retailers ('Loyal To Leominster' campaign) and the District Council (SRB funding) are examples of the types of measures which can assist in redressing the balance in favour of market towns. It remains to be seen how successful these initiatives will be in the longer term.

ASHBY-DE-LA-ZOUCH

6.89   The new Tesco store, opened in February 1996, is located at the junction with A50 and A42 on the edge of Ashby's urban area. The store occupies land that was previously identified for employment uses and is immediately adjacent to the modern industrial park, Flagstaff 42. The store carries a modern product range including in-house bakery, delicatessen and café. In addition there is a petrol filling station.

6.90   Ashby is an attractive, historic town with an urban area population of 12,295 (1991). The town is located 24 km from Leicester city centre, 10 km from Coalville and 6 km from Swadlincote. While the district has a tradition of mining industries resulting in an economic structure which has a high level of representation in manufacturing industries, the resident population is relatively affluent in comparison to the national average.

6.91   According to the CCN Lifestyle Groupings, the urban area of North West Leicestershire District (including the towns of Ashby and Coalville) has a level of representation of high income families which is almost three times the national average (27% for the district compared with 9.9% for the national average).

6.92 Ashby town centre has approximately 27,000 m^2 of net retail floorspace accommodated in 167 units. The composition of retailing in the centrew has changed little over recent years.

6.93 According to Hillier Parker's *Shopping Centres of Great Britain Classification*, Ashby has seven multiple retailers. The town's retail offer is concentrated towards day to day shopping needs. National food retailers include Somerfield, Kwik Save and Alldays. Other national multiple retailers include Boots the Chemist, WH Smith, Woolworths, Superdrug and Dorothy Perkins. In addition, the town has a number of independent retailers together with an enclosed market.

6.94 The three modern superstores in the catchment area (Tesco, Sainsbury's and Morrisons) all provide a full range of convenience goods in addition to petrol filling stations, coffee shops and in-house bakeries. The two Somerfield stores in Ashby and Swadlincote do not carry a comparable range of products and services although the stores provide an acceptable offer for their size.

6.95 The introduction of the new Tesco store has significantly increased Ashby's overall market share within its catchment area. The market shares for food stores in Swadlincote and Coalville (i.e. including town centre and out-of-centre stores) have also increased indicating that the catchment area for these stores has become more concentrated. Therefore, the new Tesco store has been able to claw back expenditure which was previously being spent outside Ashby's primary catchment area.

6.96 The market share for the Somerfield store in Ashby has remained unchanged after the Tesco opening. However, the store manager reports a 20%-25% impact. The household survey reveals that 32% of Tesco shoppers previously shopped at Somerfield. We consider the relatively short period, less than 18 months, after the store opening has not been sufficiently long for shopping patterns to settle down to allow the household survey to properly assess the store's impact.

6.97 Tesco's location out-of-centre means it caters predominantly for car borne shoppers. In contrast, respondents using the town centre Somerfield store exhibit a more diverse modal split.

Table 12 **Main Foodstore Provision – Ashby-de-la-Zouch**			
Store	Location	Size (m^2 net)	Opening Date
Kwik Save	Market Street, Ashby (town centre)	210	–
Somerfield	Derby Street, Ashby (town centre)	1,682	1984
Tesco	Resolution Road, Ashby (town centre)	2,773	February 1996
Somerfield	High Street, Swadlincote (town centre)	1,682	1994
Sainsbury	Civic Way, Swadlincote) (town centre)	1,865	1994
Co-op Extra superstore	Ridge Road, (town centre)	1,386	1993
Morrisons	Whitwick Road, Coalville (out-of-town)	3,976	1990
Source: IGD, Retailer Figures			

Similarly, respondents using the new Tesco store undertake fewer linked trips in comparison to those using the Somerfield store in Ashby town centre.

6.98   Based on an assessment of shopping patterns before and after the Tesco opening, we consider that the store has resulted in a reduction in travel distances for main food shopping. In addition, the significant level of clawback achieved by this store has resulted in an increase in the level of patronage of Ashby town centre stores for non-food shopping.

6.99   Our analysis of the household survey, discussions with retailers in Ashby, and an analysis of the indicators contained in PPG6 indicates that the Tesco opening has not materially adversely affected the vitality and viability of Ashby town centre. Nonetheless, Boots has indicated that their town centre store witnessed an adverse impact of 5.71% in terms of sales following the opening of Tesco. This suggests that whilst Ashby town centre remains vital and viable, some individual comparison retailers are likely to have been adversely affected.

6.98   On the basis of a street survey, the town has maintained its overall composition and the number of vacancies has actually reduced since the Tesco opening. The changes that have occurred in the primary frontage, (where the number of vacancies has actually increased) can be accounted for by national trends.

6.100   Therefore, we consider that the new Tesco has not had a detrimental impact on Ashby town centre. The store appears to have clawed back some trade to the town resulting in some additional linked trips to Ashby for non-food shopping purposes, although there is no evidence that the vitality and viability of the centre has been enhanced by the development.

CHAPTER 7
The District Centre Case Studies

7.1 The district centre case studies employ the same methodology as the market town studies, described in the last chapter. Three district centres were examined: Northfield in the West Midlands; Ferndown in Dorset; and Portchester in Hampshire.

NORTHFIELD

7.2 The new Safeway superstore fronts onto the A38 (Bristol Road South) which links the store to Rubery village centre, a linear High Street dominated by independent convenience retailers. The new store is approximately $3^1/_2$ km from Northfield district centre which also fronts onto the A38. The new store opened in March 1995 and provides the most up to date retail facilities in South Birmingham. The store has an in-store bakery, delicatessen and fresh fish counter, together with an in-house pharmacy, coffee shop and dry cleaners.

Northfield district centre.

7.3   The Northfield Constituency Area, within which Northfield district centre lies, is located to the south of Birmingham and is dominated by the Longbridge Rover car park. The district centre has a catchment area of approximately 54,661 people in 1991 and represents one of the larger district centres within the Birmingham conurbation. Birmingham's tradition of manufacturing industries is reflected in the numbers employed in manufacturing ($1^1/_2$ times the national average) and a consequentially low level of representation in the service sectors such as banking and finance.

7.4   Northfield district centre has approximately 47,016 m² gross of retail floorspace, comprised of 172 units. The centre includes a mix of purpose built and converted retail properties on both sides of the A38 – Bristol Road South. The centre is focused upon a purpose built enclosed shopping centre (The Grosvenor Centre) which was constructed in the 1970s and incorporates a multi-storey car park. The Grosvenor Centre has a number of national multiple retailers including Sainsbury, Iceland and Clarke's shoes. The other retail units in the district centre include a dated Tesco store, Boots the Chemist, Dixons, together with a number of High Street banks. The distribution of foodstores in the immediate area is set out in Table 13.

7.5   The Sainsbury store in Northfield district centre provides a comprehensive range of

convenience goods but lacks room for other facilities such as in-store bakeries and delicatessens, or coffee shops. The Tesco store in Northfield is small and dated and only carries a limited range of goods.

7.6   The relatively short period since the Safeway opening presents difficulties in measuring the store's impact. Many affected retailers will continue trading in the expectation of improved performance before finally closing.

7.7   The new Safeway store has increased market share in the defined catchment area by 25%. The store has drawn the majority of its trade from existing foodstores in Northfield and in particular, the Sainsbury in The Grosvenor Shopping Centre. However, according to our survey, this store has increased its market share in other parts of the study area, and overall has increased its market share over the study period.

7.8   The survey indicates that the market share of stores in Rubery has fallen by 25% impact overall. Rubery has maintained its principal foodstore retailers (including SoLo, Kwik Save and Co-op Pioneer) but has lost one of the three independent greengrocers and two of its five independent butchers.

7.9   Since the opening of the new store, the frequency of visits to Northfield for main food

Table 13 **Main Foodstore Provision – Northfield**			
Store	Location	Size (m² net)	Opening Date
Sainsbury	Northfield district centre	2,322	January 1993
Tesco	Northfield district centre	686	August 1970
Safeway	Rubery – Bristol Road South	3,252	March 1995
Sainsbury	Selly Oak district centre	2,825	June 1986
Kwik Save	Rubery village centre	1,412	Existing
SoLo	Rubery village centre	446	Existing
Co-op Pioneer	Rubery village centre	465	Existing
Source: IGD and Hillier Parker			

shopping has increased. A number of Safeway shoppers continue to use Northfield for both food and non-food purchases. The survey demonstrates that a significant number of Safeway shoppers continue to use Rubery village centre and the frequency of visits to this centre for main food shopping has not changed materially.

7.10   Safeway's relative isolation from existing retail facilities means a significant number of trips (68%) are for a single purpose and not linked in any way. Linked trips to Northfield District Centre by Safeway shoppers do not exhibit the same diverse range of activities compared with main food shoppers using Sainsbury's at Northfield. Additionally, Safeway shoppers no longer visit Northfield as frequently for non food shopping.

7.11   The assessment of indicators of vitality and viability has not illustrated any significant change in health of Northfield District Centre as a result of the new store. Whilst the levels of vacancies have increased to exceed the national average in 1997, we consider this is unrelated to the store opening. The decline of the more peripheral parts of Northfield is a trend exhibited by many suburban district centres where the number of independent retailers has declined as a result of competition from national multiple retailers.

7.12   Rubery has suffered a decline in the number of independent convenience goods retailers, and an increase in vacancies. The loss of convenience retailers may result in the long term decline of the centre unless they are replaced by other uses that attract equal levels of footfall. Currently many convenience uses have been replaced by charity shops and other uses that fail to act as a significant shopper attraction.

7.13   Rubery village centre now appears vulnerable as it lacks a sufficiently strong retail offer to underpin the health of the centre. The local traders and the local Council are now proposing (but only partly in response to the Safeway opening) a series of environmental improvements to enhance the centre.

7.14   Overall, we consider that the full effects of the Safeway opening have not been reflected in changes in the composition of both Northfield district and Rubery village centres. The household survey has shown that the Sainsbury store at Northfield has maintained its market share while other smaller stores such as the Tesco at Northfield and other foodstores in Rubery have experienced significant decline. Based on the evidence of the household survey, we consider that Northfield district centre will maintain its vitality and viability although its prime retail frontage will become increasingly concentrated as peripheral locations decline.

7.15   This decline is only partly attributed to the Safeway store opening. Northfield district centre has a significant number of independent retailers which have nationally experienced a decline as a result of the increasing competition from large food superstores both in town centre and out-of-centre locations. The extent of impact on Rubery village centre recorded by the household survey indicates that there are likely to be store closures amongst the remaining foodstores in the near future. As this centre is dependent upon its convenience offer, these closures could undermine the centre's long term vitality and viability.

FERNDOWN

7.16   In August 1994, Sainsbury opened a superstore approximately one mile to the west of Ferndown District Centre. The store is located on the A31 Ringwood Road, and has a frontage of approximately 350 m. It is therefore highly visible to passing traffic.

7.17   Ferndown is a district centre and the largest settlement in East Dorset, with an urban area population of 25,258. It is located on the A31 trunk road, and is approximately 8 miles north of Bournemouth; eight miles north-east of Poole; and six miles east of Wimborne.

Ferndown district centre.

7.18   Ferndown has a below average proportion of employment in manufacturing, although the Ferndown and Uddens industrial estates to the north-west of the district centre are important centres of employment. The district centre has a significantly higher proportion of employment in distribution, hotels and catering than the national average (30.7% compared with 21.5%). Similarly, it has a relatively strong provision of banking, finance and business services.

7.19   According to the CCN Lifestyle groupings, Ferndown is a relatively affluent centre with a significantly higher proportion of high income families compared with the national average (27.1% compared with 9.9%). The unemployment rate in Ferndown in April 1996 was 7.4%, compared with the national average of 7.8%.

7.20   Ferndown has approximately 28,177 m^2 of gross floorspace comprising 112 street level retail units. According to Hillier Parker's *Shopping Centres of Great Britain Classification*, Ferndown has a modest multiple count of four, including Boots, Superdrug and Adams Childrenswear. Nonetheless, in the context of a district centre, Ferndown provides a reasonably comprehensive range of mainstream comparison retailers; albeit the majority of which are operated by independents.

7.21   Ferndown is served by a range of small independent food retailers and larger national foodstores. The latter includes a Tesco superstore, which forms an integral part of the Ferndown Centre, Kwik Save and Iceland. The provision of main foodstores serving Ferndown is summarised in Table 14.

Table 14 Main Foodstore Provision – Ferndown			
Store	**Location**	**Size (m² net)**	**Opening Date**
Tesco	Penny walk, Ferndown (town centre)	3,189	November 1995
Sainsbury	Ringwood Road, Ferndown (out-of-centre)	2,993	August 1994
Kwik Save	Ringwood Road, Ferndown	557	–
Iceland	Victoria Road, Ferndown (town centre)	508	–
Waitrose	The Furlong Ringwood (town centre)	1,387	August 1991
Safeway	Meeting House Lane, Ringwood (town centre)	1,745	November 1983
Source: IGD			

7.22   The out-of-centre Sainsbury on Ringwood Road is slightly smaller than the Tesco in Ferndown itself. Nonetheless, the Sainsbury provides a full range of convenience products (including bakery, fresh meat and cheese counters) as well as restaurant, petrol filling station and cash point banking facilities. Immediately adjoining the Sainsbury is a Boots Chemist.

7.23   The out-of-centre Sainsbury has increased the total convenience goods market share of Ferndown, and reduced the market share of the district centre itself. Following the opening of Sainsbury, the Safeway supermarket in the district centre closed. Whilst this was part of a nationwide programme of store closures undertaken by Safeway in respect of some of their smaller and more dated stores, the opening of the out-of-centre Sainsbury is likely to have contributed towards Safeway's closure.

7.24   The out-of-centre Sainsbury has not materially increased the catchment area of Ferndown, nor has it severely constrained the catchment area of the principal foodstore in the district centre itself (Tesco). However, it has been relatively successful in clawing back trade from competing centres, for example, 6% of Sainsbury's shoppers previously used foodstores in Ringwood; 11% previously used foodstores in Poole; and 4%

of shoppers previously used foodstores in Verwood and Wimborne. In contrast, the store has been relatively unsuccessful in clawing back trade from Bournemouth, reflecting the relatively dense concentration of large foodstores in and around Bournemouth.

7.25   Whilst Tesco in the Ferndown district centre witnessed the single greatest impact, this was to some extent mitigated by the transference of trade from the closure of Safeway in the district centre. The pattern of frequency of visits and the proportion of total food expenditure spent in the store has remained largely unchanged; further evidence that Tesco continues to perform the role of the main food shopping destination.

7.26   We understand that the Kwik Save discount store in the district centre is to close. Again, this is part of a rationalisation process currently being undertaken by the company in respect of 107 of their smaller and more dated stores. The agents acting for Kwik Save indicate that in their view the store's imminent closure is not directly related to any fall in turnover as a result of Sainsbury.

7.27   Our discussions with some of the smaller convenience retailers in the district centre suggest that a large number of these have witnessed a decline in turnover since Sainsbury opened.

Whilst all considered that the opening of Sainsbury was a contributory factor, they also acknowledged that the general economic recession and the relaxation of Sunday trading laws had also been key factors. In terms of comparison retailers, our research suggests that whilst a number have witnessed a decline in their turnover during the last two years, few considered that the opening of Sainsbury was the principal reason. However, a number considered that the closure of Safeway and the subsequent drop in pedestrian footfall along Victoria Road had adversely affected a number of comparison retailers who rely on passing trade.

7.28   In terms of the modal split, the effect of the opening of Sainsbury has been broadly neutral. It is probable that those respondents in the survey who currently drive to the Sainsbury store, also used to drive to their previous main food shopping destination. The use of public transport (bus) is very low, reflecting the generally poor provision of public transport in Ferndown and the surrounding areas, and the generally high car ownership levels.

7.29   There does not appear to have been any substantive change in the propensity to undertake linked shopping trips on the part of Sainsbury shoppers. The Sainsbury store generates a relatively low proportion of linked trips, although this is not surprising as the store is located one mile to the east of the centre, while the main employment areas and schools are located to the west. There does, however, appear to have been a decline in the frequency of visits to Ferndown district centre on the part of Sainsbury's customers. This is not surprising given that a large proportion of Sainsbury's customers previously shopped at Tesco, and so no longer need to go to the district centre for their main food shopping.

7.30   Whilst there is likely to have been a slight reduction in the distance travelled by Sainsbury's shoppers due to the limited transfer of trade from other centres (e.g. Poole and Ringwood), some 40% of Sainsbury's customers live outside the Ferndown area, and may therefore have to travel further than prior to the opening of Sainsbury. Therefore, it is likely that the overall change in travel distance since the opening of Sainsbury is broadly neutral.

Ferndown out-of-centre Sainsbury.

7.31 There has been no clearly discernible change in the diversity of uses or representation of retailers in the district centre since Sainsbury opened. While there has been some shift in the representation of individual sectors of comparison retailers, there is no indication of any deterioration in the overall provision. Similarly, our analysis of other relevant PPG6 indicators suggest that the vitality and viability of Ferndown district centre has not been undermined by the out-of-centre Sainsbury.

PORTCHESTER

7.32 The new Tesco store at North Harbour is adjacent to the junction of the A27 and M27 near Portsmouth and opened in August 1995. The store is immediately adjacent to a number of residential properties and forms part of a mixed use development area known as Port Solent comprising a marina, hotel, cinema and residential properties. The store carries a modern product range including in-house bakery, delicatessen and coffee shop. In addition, there is a petrol filling station on the site.

7.33 Portchester is focused on a purpose built district centre including a pedestrianised shopping precinct on West Street. Further retail units lie to the west of the main precinct including a number of converted and purpose built shop units. Portchester is 3 km from the Tesco superstore at North Harbour, and is 5 km from Cosham, a small district centre, 6 km from Fareham and 9 km from Portsmouth city centre. The urban area of Portchester had a population of 28,611 in 1991. It is difficult to provide a clear picture of the demographic and socio-economic profile of Portchester's catchment area as it straddles the administrative districts of both Portsmouth City and Fareham Borough Council.

7.34 Portchester district centre is surrounded by high density residential properties and the centre itself includes a mix of uses including a health centre, library and church. The centre's main foodstore is Somerfield on West Street. There is a weekly market held along the length of the pedestrian precinct including stalls selling fresh vegetables, fish and meat in addition to household items, clothing and electrical goods. The centre is well provided for with free surface level car parking

Table 15 Main Foodstore Provision – Portchester

Store	Location	Size (m² net)	Opening Date
Somerfield	12 West Street, Portchester (district centre)	823	–
Iceland	34-36 West Street, Portchester (district centre)	–	–
Co-op Community Store	248 White Hart Lane, Portchester (local shopping parade)	294	–
Tesco	Clement Attlee Way, North Harbour, Portsmouth (out-of-centre)	4,383	August 1995
Sainsbury's	Fitzherbert Road, nr Cosham, Portsmouth (out-of-centre)	3,169	May 1992
Asda	Speedfields Industrial Park, Fareham (out-of-centre)	5,256	February 1990
Sainsbury's	Broadcut, Fareham (out-of-centre)	2,639	July 1993
Tesco	16 High Street, Cosham (out-of-centre)	1,389	October 1980

Source: IGD, Retailer figures

and there is a purpose built bus stop outside the Somerfield foodstore.

7.35　We estimate that the retail floorspace of the district centre is in the region of 7,250 m^2 accommodated in 69 units. Multiple retailers in the centre include Iceland, Threshers Off licence and a Superdrug chemists. The centre is dominated by convenience and service uses including hairdressers, estate agents and two national high street banks.

7.36　The Somerfield store at Portchester provides a reasonable product offer given its size, but lacks the range of facilities found in the other nearby superstores. In particular, the out-of-centre Asda and Sainsbury's stores at Fareham, the Sainsbury's store near Cosham together with to the Tesco at North Harbour all provide a full range of convenience goods and coffee shops, in-house bakeries and petrol filling stations.

7.37　The new Tesco store at North Harbour has increased market share in the Portchester catchment area, although it does not appear to have had any adverse impact on the market share of the Somerfield store in Portchester district centre. This store has actually increased its market share from 1% to 4% since the store opening. Despite this apparent increase in market share the Store Manager reports that the new Tesco store has curtailed any growth in the store's turnover, resulting in a 2%-3% impact.

7.38　The Tesco store has drawn the majority of its trade from other similar superstores in the catchment area. These include the two modern stores in Fareham (Sainsbury's and Asda) and the new Sainsbury's on Fitzherbert Road near Cosham.

7.39　The location of the Tesco store means it caters predominantly for car borne shoppers. The proportion of visits by bus is particularly low; a function of the frequency of direct bus services to the store. More significantly, however, the survey indicates there has been an overall increase in the use of the car for main food shopping trips.

7.40　The survey has shown that Tesco shoppers (North Harbour) exhibit a higher propensity to undertake linked trips compared with other case study towns. For example, 65% of Tesco respondents undertake linked trips (compared with 63% for Leominster). There has been a slight reduction in distance travelled for main food shopping. However, this is offset by an increase in the frequency of main food shopping and an increase in the use of the car. Therefore, we conclude that the new store has not resulted in a reduction in travel distances.

7.41　We have been unable to draw any substantive conclusions on Tesco's impact on the vitality and viability of Portchester district centre having regard to the indicators set out in Figure 1 of PPG6. The district centre has retained its two main foodstores (Somerfield and Iceland), and no store closures are directly attributable to the store opening. Comments made by local retailers indicate that the range of facilities at Portchester are in decline, illustrated by the recent closure of a national high street bank, resulting in a reduction in pedestrian flows in the centre. However, we do not consider Tesco has had a significant adverse impact upon Portchester.

sector investment that may be required to counteract the loss of market share in the town centre (e.g. decline in state of town centre environment).

(c)   Retailer/Investor Confidence

8.36   Whilst most of the case study towns/district centres have witnessed some change in the diversity of uses and representation of retailers, Fakenham and Leominster appear to have witnessed the most significant change. They have seen a deterioration in the range of specialist convenience retailers as well as a decline in the range of quality comparison retailers. Both currently have vacancy levels in excess of the national average, in contrast to the situation prior to the opening of the out-of-centre superstores. This is indicative of a general decline not only in the confidence of existing retailers, but also a reluctance on the part of new retailers, particularly multiples, to be represented in these centres.

8.37   In recognition of the lack of retailer/investor confidence in the town centre, retailers in Leominster have set up the 'Loyal To Leominster' campaign to generate greater confidence in the business community in an attempt to attract shoppers back to the town centre and in turn, create a more positive image to potential new retailers. In the first year of the scheme, at least 25% of participating retailers witnessed a material improvement in their turnover. In addition, there are recent signs of an attempt to develop a more specialist shopping function in Leominster by encouraging antiques and craft retailers to capitalise on the town's reputation as an antiques and craft centre. This type of initiative, which seeks to develop the strengths of market towns and create a 'competitive advantage', is likely, if sustained and successful, to engender greater retailer and investor confidence.

8.38   Similar initiatives have been set up in other market towns, including the 'Cirencester First' campaign, which was instigated by retailers in Cirencester town centre specifically to combat competition from out-of-town retailing. These types of initiatives tend to be initiated by retailers'/traders' associations, and whilst they can and do fulfil an important function, they are generally a reactive response to a perceived threat, rather than part of a wider pro-active strategy for the market towns/district centres.

8.39   The significant increase in the number of town centre managers since the formation of the Association of Town Centre Management (ATCM) in 1991 reflects the growing awareness of the benefits of a more pro-active, structured, and wide-ranging body to co-ordinate the disparate interests of town centres. However, as many market towns and district centres are relatively small both in physical and population size, they do not generally have or could reasonably justify individual town centre managers/strategies; although a single town centre manager responsible for a number of small towns in a particular area can work successfully. None of our case study towns/centres has a town centre manager, although in St Neots we understand that one is soon to be appointed.

8.40   Whilst we support fully the concept of Town Centre Management, we consider that it is the responsibility of the local authority through the Development Plan to recognise the strengths and weaknesses of the market towns/district centres within its jurisdiction, and to devise appropriate pro-active strategies to improve them. Town Centre Management may, depending on the size and function of the town/centre concerned, be an appropriate adjunct to the development plan strategy, but should not be seen as a substitute for it.

8.41   Our research also suggests that even the threat of an out-of-centre foodstore can have an adverse effect on retailer confidence. For example, our discussions with local traders and the Chamber of Trade and Commerce in Fakenham indicate that whilst the Safeway application was being considered by the District Council there was a decline in business confidence. Our analysis of other case study towns, appeal decisions and our experience as practitioners suggests that this type of response from retailers is not unique to Fakenham.

(d)   Employment

8.42   As part of our analysis of economic impacts, we have attempted in the case studies to identify changes in employment levels in retailing as a consequence of the opening of large foodstores.

The principal difficulty we have encountered is the lack of accessible, up to date, and comprehensive employment data. Our discussions with district Councils, TEC's, employment bureaux and Nomis has highlighted the particular difficulties in attempting to analyse employment data on a town/district centre basis.

8.43   We have contacted a range of food retailers in each of the case study towns centres to assess the change in employment levels following the development of large foodstores. Whilst some were able to provide piecemeal data, most were unable to identify previous levels of employment, and we have therefore been unable to determine the net change. Nonetheless from our discussions with retailers, a superstore of 2,322 m^2 net typically provides between 125 and 206 full-time equivalent jobs. In the case of Sainsbury's store at Ferndown, 65 full-time and 300 part-time staff are employed, equating to a full-time equivalent of 206 employees.

8.44   Whilst it is possible that jobs created by the new large foodstores may have in some of the case study market towns and district centres (e.g. Ferndown) offset any fall in employment in retailing which may have occurred, it is important that the effects on other related businesses are also taken account of. In particular, job losses in retailing can have implications for the distribution sector, as well as the professional services sector (e.g. local accountants and tax advisors).

8.45   According to Business Monitor SDA25, employment in retail businesses nationally has remained relatively static (2.33 million in 1986 as compared with 2.38 million in 1994). This suggests that notwithstanding the significant increase in the number of superstores during this period, a large proportion of which in out-of-centre locations, there has not been any major increase in the level of employment in retail businesses during this period. This contrasts to the significant increase in the turnover of grocery stores during the same period. This suggests that as a sector, retailing has become more efficient, with fewer employees achieving a higher level of sales. It also suggests that there has been some sectoral shift in employment in favour of out-of-centre locations.

8.46   Whilst recent research undertaken by Boots the Chemist on behalf of the National Retail Planning Forum concludes that there is clear evidence that new superstores have, on average, a negative effect on retail employment, our own research has failed to demonstrate any conclusive evidence of any significant positive or negative effect on the wider local economy as a result of new foodstore openings.

To What Extent Do Large Foodstores Claw Back Expenditure From Competing Centres?

(a)   Claims by Foodstore Retailers

8.47   A common claim put forward by foodstore operators at Public Inquiries is that large edge-of-centre/out-of-centre foodstores compete principally with other comparable facilities rather than with smaller town centre foodstores. In addition, they claim that these stores claw back expenditure leaking to more distant competing centres, and by so doing increase the opportunities, particularly for edge-of-centre stores, for linked shopping trips. A counter view is that whilst superstores may claw back some expenditure, they also compete directly with town centre supermarkets, and also absorb some of the 'top-up' trade of specialist convenience retailers.

(b)   Factors Influencing Levels of Clawback

8.48   The results of our case studies suggest that the location of large foodstores (edge-of-centre and out-of-centre) and the nature of the catchment area do make a quantifiable difference in terms of the extent of clawback. In Cirencester, the principal effect of the edge-of-centre Waitrose has been to transfer trade from the old town centre Waitrose to the new store. It has not 'clawed back' any significant levels of trade from outside the immediate catchment area of the town; those who previously used foodstores in Cheltenham, Gloucester and Swindon have not materially altered their main food shopping patterns.

8.49   The store has not therefore extended Cirencester's catchment beyond that already secured by the larger and more accessible (by car) out-of-centre Tesco; neither has it diverted any significant proportion of trade from the out-of-centre Tesco into the centre. One likely reason for this lack of clawback achieved by Waitrose is the already significant alteration of food shopping patterns as a result of the out-of-centre Tesco. There is no evidence to suggest any additional 'spin-off' non-food trade being secured as a consequence of the new Waitrose. In this respect, the store appears to have had little if any discernible positive impact on the town centre.

8.50   Similarly, the edge-of-centre Safeway in Warminster has not increased materially the extent of Warminster's catchment, and in particular has not clawed back, as one might have expected, any significant trade from modern foodstores in Frome (Sainsbury) and from Trowbridge (Asda and Tesco). The store has drawn most of its trade from the old Safeway and Gateway stores in the town centre. While the overall convenience goods market share of Warminster increased from 20% to 25% following the opening of Safeway, the market share of town centre food retailers declined from 20% to 5%.

8.51   The Chamber of Trade considers that a new pedestrian flow has been established between the Safeway and the prime shopping area of the town centre. However, there is limited evidence from our analysis that this has secured any significant benefits for the town centre by way of additional expenditure in the comparison and service sectors. Like Cirencester, this store appears to have generated few if any positive benefits to the existing town centre.

8.52   In terms of out-of-centre foodstores, these have in general been more successful at clawing back trade from competing centres. For example, in Fakenham some 46% of the trade of the out-of-centre Safeway is derived from clawback of expenditure. Similarly, in Leominster a large proportion of the trade of the out-of-centre Safeway is derived from clawback from competing centres such as Hereford. This suggests that shoppers who were already using large out-of-centre foodstores are willing to transfer their trade to a closer store.

8.53   Notwithstanding these levels of clawback, both Fakenham and Leominster have witnessed a significant decline in their town centre market shares. We consider that both centres have been adversely affected by the out-of-centre foodstores. Notwithstanding any savings in overall trip lengths, considered later, the clawback to out-of-centre foodstores has led to no tangible benefit in either centre.

8.54   Other case studies also suggest out-of-centre superstores have clawed back significant amounts of trade. For example, in St Neots, the out-of-centre Tesco has clawed back high levels of expenditure previously leaking to Bedford and Huntingdon. Similarly, the out-of-centre Safeway in Ferndown has clawed back relatively high levels of trade, particularly from large foodstores in the nearby centres of Poole and Ringwood. The distribution of trade for these centres reflects two factors. First, the largest single source of trade diversion tends to be from the largest nearest store catering for bulk food purchases. Second, it highlights that those shoppers who already choose to use large out-of-centre foodstores in nearby centres, are generally willing to transfer their trade to a closer store to their place of residence. In the case of St Neots, in the majority of cases these are operated by the same retailer (Tesco).

8.55   In contrast, the out-of-centre Safeway close to Northfield district centre has proved to be less successful in clawing back large amounts of trade from competing centres. This reflects the dense concentration of large foodstores in the Birmingham urban area, and the relatively tightly defined yet overlapping catchment areas of individual district centres within it. This is generally a distinguishing feature of district centres and highlights not only some of the problems in defining what constitutes a district centre, but also analysing what can be particularly complex shopping patterns.

8.56   On the basis of the case studies, there appears to be some difference in the ability of edge-of-centre and out-of-centre foodstores to claw back significant amounts of trade from competing centres. In the case of edge-of-centre stores, there appears to be a greater propensity to transfer trade from the town centre to an edge-of-centre location rather than to claw back expenditure from outside the immediate catchment area. It should be noted that in the case of the Cirencester Pilot survey, there are specific circumstances (e.g. the out-of-centre Tesco), which may in part explain the limited levels of clawback. Nonetheless, we consider that greater consideration needs to be given to the assumption implied in the sequential test of PPG6 that edge-of-centre locations are necessarily the most appropriate solution where town centre sites are not currently available.

Do Large Edge-of-centre/ Out-of-centre Foodstores Affect Travel Distances and Mode of Travel?

(a)　The Key Variables

8.57　In order to address this question we have examined the case studies and examined if any identifiable trends emerge on modal split, linked trips, frequency of visit and travel distance. Data on Cirencester is only included for some criteria since not all the questions in the pilot and main surveys are comparable.

(b)　Modal Split

8.58　When examining modal split, two comparisons have been made. The first is the mode used to access the new edge-of-centre/out-of-centre store when compared with the town centre. This gives useful data on the general relationship between location and modal choice. The second comparison focuses on the people now using the new store and whether their mode has changed. This gives a more direct measure of the impact of the new store.

8.59　Table 17 summarises the pair wise comparisons of modal choice for each of the case studies. A comparison is made between the new store, be it out-of-centre or edge-of-centre, and the main town centre food store, where applicable.

8.60　As we would have expected, in all instances where there is a town centre store, this store attracted a greater proportion of walk-in trade and a smaller proportion of car drivers. Within town centres there are many businesses and usually

residential property within walking distance of the shops. In contrast, most of the edge-of-centre/out-of-centre stores were not surrounded by significant residential areas, and thus are not generally attractive to walk-in trade.

8.61　Furthermore, as a generality, people without cars are more likely to live close to the town centre where they can access day to day facilities without recourse to a car. The surveys also showed strongly that if a car was available for food shopping then people would use it.

8.62　In general a relatively small proportion of people visited any of the stores by bus. The notable exception to this was the Sainsbury store at Northfield where 36% of customers use this mode. For market towns bus services are often relatively poor. The services generally run as a series of loops focusing on the town centre with longer distance services linking with other market towns or regional centres. There are very few cross town services. Therefore it may be possible for the majority of the population to get to the town centre by bus, but only a minority could access an out-of-centre store without a change of bus in the town centre.

8.63　Given the low frequencies of most services this makes the trip both arduous and time consuming. This fact is reflected in the very low bus usage found at the out-of-centre stores. This level of usage does not seem to be affected by the frequency of services past the store.

8.64　These results illustrate the key role town centres play in providing accessible services to those who chose not to or are unable to have access to a car for shopping. Such members of the community are likely to be best served by facilities that are grouped together and can be jointly used on one trip by bus.

8.65　Table 18 shows the change in modal split for those now using the new store under investigation. In virtually all cases there has been an increase in the number of people using their own car and a decrease in the number walking or using the bus to do their food shopping. Although not shown in the table, there has also been an increase in the number of people getting a lift to the store.

Table 17 Modal Split Comparison

Town	Store	Category	Modal Split (%)			
			Own Car	Bus	Walk	Other
Ashby de la Zouch	Tesco	Out-of-centre	93	2	1	4
	Somerfield	Town Centre	54	5	35	6
Cirencester	Tesco	Out-of-centre	93	0	0	6
	Waitrose	Edge-of-centre	89	2	4	5
	Tesco	Town Centre	57	6	21	16
Fakenham	Safeway	Out-of-centre	93	0	1	6
	Budgens	Town Centre	53	9	29	9
Ferndown	Sainsbury	Out-of-centre	92	1	3	4
	Tesco	Town Centre	83	2	12	3
Leominster	Safeway	Out-of-centre	90	0	4	6
	Somerfield	Town Centre	59	6	20	15
Northfield	Safeway	Out-of-centre	86	4	6	4
	Sainsbury	District Centre	40	36	14	10
Portchester	Tesco	Out-of-centre	89	1	7	7
	Sainsbury	Out-of-centre (Cosham)	93	0	5	2
St Neots	Tesco	Out-of-centre	86	1	3	10
	Waitrose	Town Centre	64	5	18	13
Warminster	Safeway	Edge-of-centre	77	1	16	6
	Sainsbury	Out-of-centre (Frome)	80	0	3	17

Source: Intermarket Research Household Interview Survey (1996/1997)

8.66   Although the percentage differences are relatively small, the consistency of the results suggests a trend is being measured. The switch from walk mode to car could be for a number of reasons. Perhaps the most likely is that people who used to walk to a town centre store near where they lived now elect to drive to the new store by car. This could reflect the general trend towards undertaking more food shopping on a bulk basis by car. It may also be that the opening of a new store is the catalyst for people's change in food shopping habits. Additionally, the generally later opening hours of superstores may encourage more shopping in the evening when a car is available and therefore can be used for food shopping.

Table 18 Change in Modal Split

Town (New Edge/ Out-of-centre Store	Modal Split (%)								
	Own Car			Bus			Walk		
	Before	After	Change	Before	After	Change	Before	After	Change
Ashby-de-la-Zouch (Tesco)	91	93	+2	3	2	-1	3	1	-2
Fakenham (Safeway)	90	93	+3	2	0	-2	5	1	-4
Ferndown (Sainsbury)	90	92	+2	3	1	-2	4	3	-1
Leominster (Safeway)	84	90	+6	3	0	-3	11	4	-5
Northfield (Safeway)	80	86	+6	5	4	-1	10	6	-4
Portchester (Tesco)	78	85	+7	5	1	-4	15	7	-8
St Neots (Tesco)	84	86	+2	4	1	-3	5	3	-2
Warminster (Safeway)	80	77	-3	1	1	0	15	16	+1

Source: Intermarket Research Household Interview Survey (1996/1997)

(c)   Car Availability

8.67   The change in the availability of a car to undertake the main food shopping is shown in Table 19.

Table 19 Change in Car Availability

Town	Store	Before			After			Change		
		Yes	No	Varies	Yes	No	Varies	Yes	No	Varies
Ashby-de-la-Zouch	Tesco	89	11	1	82	13	5	-7	+2	+4
Fakenham	Safeway	93	6	1	89	7	4	-4	+1	+3
Ferndown	Sainsbury	92	7	1	91	7	2	-1	0	+1
Leominster	Safeway	89	1	*	86	12	2	-3	+1	+2
Northfield	Safeway	76	23	1	70	24	6	-6	+1	+5
Portchester	Tesco	84	15	2	80	16	4	-4	+1	+2
St Neots	Tesco	93	7	0	89	8	3	-4	+1	+3
Warminster	Safeway	87	12	1	85	11	4	-2	-1	+3

* = less than 0.5%

Source: Intermarket Research Household Interview Survey (1996/1997)

8.68   In all cases the results show car availability now is less than before the store under investigation opened. However in the before situation there are a large number of 'don't knows' and these could be distorting the situation. The results do not appear to alter the conclusions on modal split identified above since car availability is going in the opposite direction to car usage. There is a strong correlation between car availability and use for shopping trips. If people have a car available, they are likely to use it.

(d)   Combined/Linked Trips

8.69   We consider the propensity to undertake linked trips depends on four interrelated factors:-

- the extent to which the store complements the town centre/district centre;

- the distance and physical linkages between the two;

- the relative size of the centre as compared with the store; and

- accessibility, parking and orientation of the store.

8.70   Table 20 below shows the proportion of trips to a foodstore that were combined with a visit to the town centre. This means that people visited the town centre on the same trip as the foodstore. This is different from the general propensity for people to visit the town centre for food shopping whether on the same or a separate trip.

8.71   The figures show that a good degree of trip combination does take place. The town centre stores generally have the greatest proportion of people combining trips, followed by the edge-of-centre stores; the out-of-centre stores display the least linkage. This is as one would expect since, with a town centre foodstore people are already in the town centre, and are therefore more likely to undertake other activities whilst they are there

Table 20 Linked Trips (%)

Town	Out-of-centre		Edge-of-centre		Town centre	
Ashby-de-la-Zouch	Tesco	54			Somerfield	77
Fakenham	Safeway	45			Budgens	70
Ferndown	Sainsbury	51			Tesco	64
Leominster	Safeway	63			Somerfield	71
Northfield	Safeway	25			Sainsbury	64
Portchester	Tesco	65				
	Sainsbury	47				
St Neots	Tesco	37			Waitrose	79
Warminster	Sainsbury	36	Safeway	58		

Note: The figure for linked trips for the Waitrose, edge-of-centre store at Cirencester was 47% although the question was phrased slightly different.

Table 21 Change in Linked Trips (%)

Town	Store	Proportion of Linked Trips (%)		
		Before	After	Change
Ashby-de-la-Zouch	Tesco	46	54	+8
Fakenham	Safeway	55	45	-10
Ferndown	Sainsbury	48	51	+3
Leominster	Safeway	52	63	+11
Northfield	Safeway	43	25	-18
Portchester	Tesco	67	65	-2
St Neots	Tesco	47	37	-10
Warminster	Safeway	55	58	+3

Source: Intermarket Research Household Interview Survey (1996/1997)

8.72 At Warminster a significant proportion of people walked between the edge-of-centre store and the town centre. Of those who linked their trip, 80% advised that they walked. Although a similar question was not asked at Cirencester anecdotal evidence suggests very few people walk between the Waitrose and the town centre. This difference reflects the better integration between the Safeway and Warminster town centre compared with the Waitrose and Cirencester town centre. Nonetheless, we consider that even in the case of Safeway, the store is relatively poorly integrated with the town centre, as it effectively 'turns its back' on it.

8.73 There is some variability in the effect of the new stores on linking of trips (see Table 21), reflecting the differences in individual circumstances. For some of the towns, shoppers using the new store link their trips to the town centre more than previously (e.g. 52% to 63% in Leominster). This may well be because before the new store opened they were travelling to another town for their food shopping. However, there is no evidence of any significant increase in the use of centres for non-food shopping as a result. For other towns the propensity to link trips goes down probably because a more significant proportion of trade has been diverted from the town centre.

(e) Frequency of Food Shopping
8.74 Table 22 shows the frequency of main food shopping trips by those now shopping at the new store. The weighted factor is a measure showing the overall frequency. The higher the factor, the higher the frequency of visit.

8.75 As can be seen, for all the case studies except Fakenham, the change in frequency due to the opening of the new store is low, i.e. circa 5%. There does seem to be a trend towards a slight increase in frequency which could be due to the fact that some people will be travelling less far to the store and therefore may choose to shop more frequently. However, based on the evidence of this study, it is unlikely that the change in frequency will be a material factor in assessing the overall change in vehicle distance travelled.

(f) Travel Distance
8.76 Within the scope of this study a detailed quantitative assessment of the change in travel distance for each case study has not been undertaken. The task requires more data than was available and was not necessarily considered an appropriate use of resources. However, we have considered the main factors that are likely to influence travel distance and any evidence from the case studies as to how these factors have changed. This will assist local authorities in determining if a detailed assessment is appropriate in the particular circumstances they are considering.

8.77 The change in the overall distance travelled by car for food shopping as a result of a new store will be influenced by four main factors as follows:

- the difference in distance travelled to the new store compared with the previous store;

- the change in mode of travel;

- the change in frequency of food shop; and

- the change in the propensity to link trips.

Table 22 Frequency of Shopping Trips – Target Store Customers

	1 Daily (%)	2 2-3 times per week (%)	3 Weekly(%)	4 Fortnightly (%)	5 Monthly (%)	6 Weighted Factor (Number)
BEFORE NEW STORE OPENED						
Ashby-de-la-Zouch	2	21	65	11	2	534
Fakenham	6	39	51	4	0	722
Ferndown	2	18	72	4	4	520
Leominster	4	29	45	14	8	586
Northfield	3	25	59	6	7	565
Portchester	0	30	59	4	7	551
St Neots	5	15	56	18	5	515
Warminster	7	37	50	2	4	718
AFTER NEW STORE OPENED						
Ashby-de-la-Zouch	5	21	59	9	4	568
Fakenham	3	22	68	7	1	567
Ferndown	2	22	68	7	1	547
Leominster	5	23	52	15	5	573
Northfield	2	31	48	12	6	572
Portchester	1	35	45	12	7	581
St Neots	3	25	58	10	4	566
Warminster	7	44	42	7	0	762
CHANGE DUE TO NEW STORE OPENING						
Ashby-de-la-Zouch	+3	0	-6	-2	+2	+34
Fakenham	-3	-17	+17	+3	+1	-155
Ferndown	0	+4	-4	+3	-3	+27
Leominster	+1	-6	+7	+1	-3	-13
Northfield	-1	+6	-11	+6	-1	+7
Portchester	+1	+5	-14	+8	0	+30
St Neots	-2	+10	+2	-8	-1	+51
Warminster	0	+7	-8	+5	-4	+44

Source: Analysis of Intermarket Research Household Interview Surveys

8.78   The distance travelled will depend upon individual circumstances but there is evidence that, in certain cases, the distance travelled to a foodstore will decrease as people transfer from an out-of-town store further away to a new, more local store.

8.79   The evidence from this study is that for those now using the new edge-of-centre/out-of-centre foodstore, there has been a small increase in car use. This is likely to be due to a number of factors as previously described.

8.80   There is no strong evidence that, as a general rule, the frequency of food shopping will increase with the opening of a new store, although this will be very dependent on the particular circumstances.

8.81   Again, no strong trend was picked up showing that linked trips either increased or decreased substantively due to the opening of a new store.

8.82   The conclusion from the above is that travel distance analysis will vary from town to town depending upon the particular circumstances. There is evidence that in certain towns opening of a new edge-of-centre/out-of-centre foodstore will lead to clawback of trade from other stores and, on balance, lead to a reduction in overall travel distance. In other locations there may be no clawback and the increase in car use may lead to an increase in overall vehicle mileage. In both cases the changes are likely to be relatively small in the context of the overall distance travelled for food shopping.

Is There a Need for a Consistent Impact Methodology?

8.83   Our literature review and local authority and retailer surveys highlighted the shortcomings of many current approaches to assessing the impact of food superstores on market towns and district centres, and in particular the failure to date to integrate effectively retail and transportation impact assessments to provide a comprehensive evaluation of proposals in accordance with the guidance set out in PPG6 and PPG13.

8.84   Our case studies have identified clear evidence of the significant impacts large foodstores can and do have on town centre retailers, and on the overall vitality and viability of town centres. Our research, drawing on data provided by key town centre retailers as well as post-opening household interview surveys, indicates that impacts on market share ranging from 13% – 50% on established town centre foodstores are not uncommon.

8.85   We consider that calculation of predicted impact, i.e. trade diversion, is only the starting point for a proper assessment of the effects of edge-of-centre and out-of-centre superstores on market towns and district centres. In every case, it is the implications and interpretation of the forecast levels of impact which determine the acceptability or otherwise of such proposals. However, these issues are often overlooked, particularly when the respective parties fail to agree even a basic methodology.

8.86   The debate on this issue is often unproductive, uninformed and distracts those involved from the real issues. Unfortunately, as some approaches become over-complicated, unduly prescriptive or rely upon unsubstantiated assumptions, there is also a danger that the credibility of impact assessments can be undermined.

8.87   There is a pressing need for a common basis for assessment. We consider that this would assist greatly in enabling local authorities and the private sector to work together more effectively, and reduce unnecessary time and cost at public inquiries spent deliberating issues which could and should be dealt with at an earlier stage. In Chapter Nine, we evaluate the effectiveness and application of the methodology we have adopted in our case studies.

Are Smaller Centres More Vulnerable Than Larger Ones?

(a) Attributes of More Resilient Market Towns/District Centres

8.88   The case studies, together with our analysis of the local authority and retailer surveys, suggest that larger centres which are not dependent solely on food retailing, but also have a well-developed comparison and services function, tend to be less susceptible to harm from large foodstores. Similarly, those centres with a clearly defined tourist role, and which do not rely just on the expenditure of the local catchment are generally more robust (provided the tourist function is maintained).

8.89   For example, Cirencester is a centre which in addition to its convenience role has, in the context of a market town, a relatively strong provision of comparison retailing and services. It also continues to be an important agricultural centre, as well as a tourist destination in its own right. These factors have assisted the town in mitigating to some extent the effects of the out-of-centre Tesco and edge-of-centre Waitrose. Similarly, St Neots has a strong comparison retail offer in addition to a strong main food shopping provision.

8.90   The relative resilience of other case study towns including Ashby-de-la-Zouch and Warminster can also be explained partly by the role of tourism in the case of the former, and partly by the importance of the army barracks with regard the latter. These 'attributes' provide a wider and stronger economic base for the towns to function, and in our view have assisted in reducing the impact of the out-of-centre Tesco in Ashby and the edge-of-centre Safeway in Warminster.

(b) Features of More Fragile Market Towns/District Centres

8.91   In contrast, smaller market towns like Fakenham and Leominster are more dependent on their convenience shopping function, and have been less able to adjust to the transfer of food trade to less central locations. Unlike centres like St Neots, which has a large modern town centre foodstore, these centres have traditionally relied on smaller, independent foodstores – a sector which has declined dramatically. Both towns are located in relatively remote rural locations, but neither has a sufficiently diverse comparison retail provision, or performs a strong enough tourism function to have been unaffected by the development of large foodstores.

8.92   In terms of district centres, those centres with an already well developed convenience role, and underpinned by at least one relatively modern supermarket have been better placed to withstand the impact from out-of-centre foodstores. For example, Ferndown district centre has a relatively modern Tesco superstore, and Northfield district centre has a Sainsbury and Tesco supermarket. Whilst both centres witnessed a decline in their market share, both were sufficiently robust to withstand this.

8.93   In comparison, Portchester is a much smaller district centre than both Northfield and Ferndown and has a more limited convenience goods offer (Somerfield is the principal food retailer). Whilst there is some evidence from the household survey that frequency of visits to Portchester has fallen slightly, to date it appears to have remained relatively unaffected by the opening of the out-of-town Tesco at North Harbour. This is partly a reflection of the already dense network of food superstores in close proximity to the district centre, and suggests that in these circumstances, large foodstores tend to compete more directly with each other rather than with smaller foodstores.

How Effective are the PPG6 Health Check Indicators?

8.94   Our retailer survey has highlighted perceived shortcomings of some vitality and viability assessments. In particular, we agree with Somerfield's criticisms of assessments which include no time-based analysis, and rely on bland statements which provide no indication as to the economic strength of a town, or how it has changed over time.

8.95   Figure 1 of PPG6 identifies a range of indicators which are intended to provide useful base line and time series information on the economic health of town centres. However, no guidance is provided as to the relevance of particular indicators for different sizes of towns. As practitioners, our experience is that the value of some of these health check indicators is limited in the context of small market towns and district centres. This is particularly apparent when attempting to analyse the change in the economic health of a centre over a period of time. The case studies have reinforced this view.

8.96   For example, in small market towns (e.g. Fakenham) and in small district centres (e.g. Portchester), the terms of leases tend to be negotiated on the basis of an annual rent rather than in Zone A terms. Similarly, a large number of small market towns do not have an active investment market, so the analysis of an investment yield does not provide any meaningful commentary on the change in investors' perceptions.

8.97   In our experience, the most relevant and informative indicators of a change in vitality and viability of small market towns and district centres are diversity of uses, retailer representation, proportion of vacant street level property, pedestrian flows, and state of the town centre environment. However, their limitations need to be understood and care has to be taken in attributing too much significance to any one indicator. For example, in terms of retailer representation, it is not only the shift between different sectors (convenience, comparison and services) that is important, but the qualitative shift in the retailers represented; a trend towards an increased representation of discounters, temporary traders and charity shops can be indicative of a declining centre.

8.98   Similarly, vacancy levels need to be treated with care, as vacancies can arise even in the strongest towns. The lack of shop vacancies in a town is not in itself the definitive measure of the strength of the town; tenants may be 'locked into their leases' and unable to vacate until the expiry of their lease. In terms of comparing vacancy levels, we consider that this can be misleading; small market towns would normally be expected to have a lower vacancy level than larger centres. We suggest therefore that national average vacancy levels should be produced for each type of centre rather than as a single composite average.

8.99   Pedestrian flows are, by their nature, subject to numerous extraneous factors which can influence the number and patterns of movement in a town. They are only of any real benefit when undertaken on a regular, frequent and consistent basis. They can be particularly informative when analysed in conjunction with the change in the pattern of shop vacancies over a period of time.

8.100   The state of the town centre environmental quality can also be a useful guide as to the change in the economic health of town centres/district centres; a decline in the quality of the built environment can be indicative of a fall in investment on the part of both public and private sector, which in turn can be the result of a decline in retailer/investor confidence in the town centre. Like any other vitality and viability indicator, interpretation of any change can be extremely subjective, and therefore the benefit of undertaking any vitality and viability assessment is derived from considering the indicators in totality.

8.101   Having analysed the vitality and viability indicators in a range of different centres, it is clear that whilst the consequences of impact can have an almost immediate effect on town centre retailers (i.e. a fall in turnover), the implications of this can take some time to manifest themselves in an identifiable change in the vitality and viability indicators. Changes in rental levels and in investment yields are unlikely to be immediately apparent after the opening of a large foodstore. Similarly vacancy levels are unlikely to change significantly in the short term.

8.102 Our analysis suggests that the vitality and viability indicators in Figure 1 of PPG6 may not be sufficiently sensitive to measure the impact of large foodstores. Providing they are analysed consistently and on a regular basis, they can and do provide a useful measure of the change in the long-term vitality and viability of market towns and district centres. However, it is important to appreciate that in the context of particularly small market towns, not all of the indicators will be strictly relevant or informative.

8.103 We consider that to provide a clearer understanding of the likely effects of large foodstores, it is important that a vitality and viability monitoring programme in place. This will provide an accurate assessment of the particular strengths and weaknesses of a centre, and will enable the results of the pre-opening impact assessment to be considered in the context of an up to date analysis of the centre, as opposed to being considered as a 'snapshot'. Undertaken on this basis, and having careful regard to those PPG6 health check indicators most relevant to smaller centres, we consider that the current PPG6 indicators are sufficient to measure the qualitative effects of large foodstores over time.

CHAPTER 9

Combined Retail, Economic and Transportation Evaluation (CREATE)

9.1   In Chapter Eight, we identified the need for a consistent and robust impact methodology. In this section we evaluate the effectiveness of the approach we adopted in respect of the 'post-opening' assessments for the case studies, and the extent to which the approach methodology has a wider role as a 'pre-opening' evaluation, which is likely to be the most common application.

9.2   Our research suggests most practitioners advocate some form of 'step by step' approach to assessing retail impact, and assemble data, in varying degrees of detail, on a range of common issues. Definitions vary. However, a conventional 'step by step approach' to assessing the impact of a foodstore on a market town or district centre will typically comprise the following steps:-

- define study/survey area;

- determine base and design years;

- identify current and forecast population;

- calculate available and forecast convenience expenditure;

- assess current shopping patterns and turnover of established centres in base and design years;

- assess turnover and trade pattern of proposed development; and

- calculate impact on existing centres and stores at design year.

9.3   In parallel to such quantitative analysis, it is critical that a full town centre health check is carried out, showing changes in the centre's vitality and viability over time. Equally, it is critical that the qualitative effects of proposals are considered, including for example, the effect of the proposals on retailer and investor confidence.

However, for the purposes of defining the approach, we have concentrated on the main steps of the quantitative assessment.

9.4   The level of sophistication, use of actual survey data, and level of transparency of retail and transportation analysis varies considerably. However, all assessments comprise three broad elements:-

(a) **Data inputs**
The preparation of population and expenditure estimates for base and design years within a survey or study area as defined is potentially the least contentious aspect of any impact assessment. Such data is usually required to be agreed between developers/retailers and local authorities, and is generally agreed for the purposes of public inquiries. The main difficulty is consistency of data sources;

(b) **Assessing current shopping and travel patterns and the turnover of existing centres**
This element is generally more problematical; current shopping patterns may be modelled using a specially commissioned household interview survey to identify market shares; using gravity models applying theoretical relationships between different centres based on their size and relative attraction; judgement; or a combination of all of these.

In some cases, no attempt is made to model current patterns, but instead the turnover of existing centres is assessed by simply multiplying floorspace with a notional turnover per sq m; this approach may be criticised on two grounds. First, it usually builds in the unrealistic assumption that all centres are achieving similar and satisfactory sales levels at the base year. Second, by failing to model current patterns, it does not enable assessment of changes in shopping patterns as a result of the proposed development.

(c) **Estimation of the trading pattern and turnover of the proposed development**
This is normally the most contentious aspect of any impact assessment, as the turnover likely to be achieved by the proposed development, and the distribution of trade diversion from nearby centres will determine its impact. Unlike the first two elements, this cannot be measured by means of survey, but instead relies on predictions based on current shopping patterns, and evidence of similar types of development elsewhere. Accordingly, this is generally the area where there is the greatest scope for disagreement.

9.5   A further complication arises in the case of cumulative impact. Essentially, the decision as to which recent and committed foodstores should be taken into account when assessing cumulative impact is a matter for judgement and, where possible, agreement between the developer/retailer and local authority. Our research and experience of this issue suggests that where a succession of foodstores have opened, it may be appropriate to go back at least five years to assess the cumulative impact of current proposals and recent developments.

9.6   We consider further guidance on this issue is needed, possibly following further research on the issue of cumulative impact. In purely practical terms, the impact of a succession of foodstores can be assessed by the adoption of an agreed base year which pre-dates the developments to be considered. The difficulty of this approach is that it requires consideration of shopping patterns and turnovers prior to the opening of stores which may

have been trading for several years. However, we consider that such an assessment should be undertaken where cumulative impact is of concern.

9.7   For the purposes of developing a consistent approach to the Combined Retail, Economic and Transportation Evaluation (CREATE), we consider the conventional step by step approach may be usefully divided into two elements:-

- First, the measured variables, which should be capable of quantification based on survey and other data to produce a model of the current situation (which should be agreed);

- Second, assessment of the predicted changes against relevant criteria (which may not be agreed, but should be capable of sensitivity testing).

9.8   The basic steps employed using the CREATE approach are illustrated on Figure 2, and summarised below.

Measured Variables

(a)   Define Catchment Survey Area
9.9   In the absence of comprehensive coverage of regional, strategic or even district-wide retail surveys, identification of the appropriate survey/catchment area to adopt as the basis of the analysis is itself problematical. In the case of food superstores, drive time isochrones have been widely used to determine the likely extent of a proposal's catchment which, it is typically argued, would in most cases be unlikely to extend beyond a 20 minute of peak drive time isochrone. However, the potential extent of any proposal's catchment will be largely determined by the proximity of nearby centres and superstores. For example, in a densely populated urban area, a new superstore in or outside an established district centre is likely to achieve a far more tightly defined catchment area.

9.10   In practical terms, for the purposes of impact testing, the precise definition of the catchment or survey area is to some extent academic. The key consideration is that the study area, however defined, is drawn sufficiently widely to ensure that shopping and travel patterns within the likely sphere of influence of the proposal can be assessed, and the full implications of the

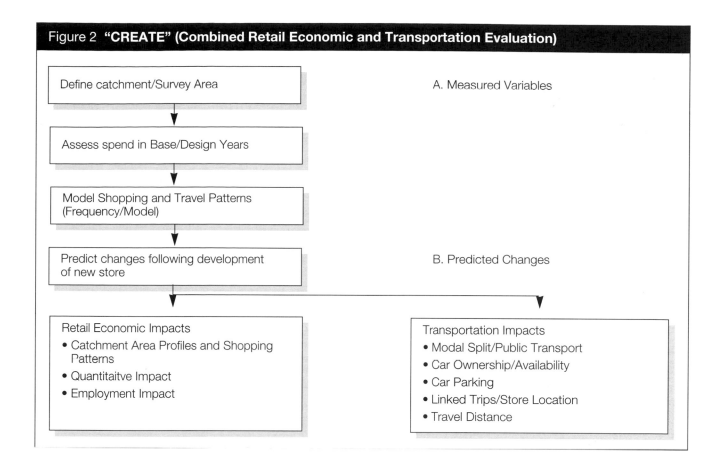

Figure 2 "CREATE" (Combined Retail Economic and Transportation Evaluation)

proposed development can be quantified. When the cumulative impact of several developments is being considered, a wider survey area may be necessary to identify the consequences of all relevant developments for the town centre(s) under consideration. It is a common criticism of retail impact assessments that they are confined to an artificially self-contained area, and have little regard to other relevant factors outside the area.

(b) Assess Population and Spend in Base/Design Years

9.11 Within the survey/catchment area as defined, population and expenditure estimates for agreed base and design years should be agreed wherever possible between retailer/developers and local authorities. To enable proper evaluation of the effects of population and expenditure growth within different parts of the survey area, these estimates should be prepared on a disaggregated basis, i.e. by breaking the study area down into pre-defined zones, either based on postcode geography or by dividing the area into separate pockets of population with their own identifiable characteristics.

9.12 Population estimates are generally available from local authorities, normally on a ward or parish basis, but rarely on a postcode sector basis. Population projections should be available on a district wide basis, but care is required when projecting population growth within different parts of the study area, whether using local authority statistics or external data sources such as the Unit for Retail Planning Information (URPI) Limited, to reflect major housing allocations or other local variations.

9.13 Per capita expenditure estimates are generally commissioned from external sources such as URPI, either on a convenience goods or business base. Practitioners have mixed views as to which is the most appropriate basis to adopt, which to some extent depends upon local circumstances. However, it is critical that a consistent approach is agreed by relevant parties. The same applies to the use of appropriate growth rates, and consistent use of constant price bases.

(c)   Model Current Patterns

9.14   We consider the best way of identifying current shopping and travel patterns is by way of a household interview survey. This should be undertaken by an independent market research company, employ a reliable sample size, and wherever possible be undertaken on the basis of a questionnaire and specification drawn up jointly between applicant and local authority. There are a growing number of examples of retailers and developers co-operating with local authorities on this issue.

9.15   Convenience shopping patterns are complex; many shoppers undertake a separate main food shop, and use other local convenience stores for everyday and top up food shopping. Surveys should be designed to identify these factors. It may not always be possible or appropriate to model shopping patterns based on survey material alone; an element of judgement is still likely to be required. However, we consider the use of surveys still offers material advantages over alternative gravity modelling techniques, or use of unsubstantiated judgements.

9.16   The level of complexity of the analysis, the number of zones used, and the extent to which individual stores or small centres are modelled explicitly will depend upon the purpose to which the analysis is being carried out, the complexity of the catchment, and the nature of the issues involved. However, we consider such analysis should be undertaken on a sufficiently disaggregated basis to highlight the main characteristics of current shopping and travel patterns, and enable the likely changes to be readily identified.

(d)   Model Turnover and Trading Pattern of Proposed Development

9.17   Based on modelled shopping patterns, the analysis should identify the total convenience turnover of existing main foodstores, and other convenience retail facilities, both in the base year, and, taking account of forecast population and expenditure growth, in the design year without the effects of the new store. If a cumulative impact assessment is being undertaken, this analysis should identify the extent to which recent developments and outstanding commitments are likely to reduce the turnover of existing centres by the design year, to enable consideration of the cumulative effects of the proposals.

9.18   Assessment of the current turnover of existing convenience stores within the study area provides a means of assessing whether current turnovers are sufficient to maintain the viability of existing centres, and where particular retailers and/or centres are likely to be vulnerable to the impact of a new store. The principal difficulty in applying such judgements is the lack of reliable benchmarks, particularly against which to compare the trading performance of local independent convenience retailers. In the case of national superstore operators, published average sales densities enable comparison of retailers' likely performance against their national average sales levels. However, local considerations should be taken into account when assessing the significance of retailers' performance against national average figures.

PREDICTED CHANGES

9.19   In analysing the results of the Pilot Study of Cirencester, we developed a range of criteria, employed subsequently in the eight case studies, which we consider provides a robust and comprehensive framework for assessing the likely consequences of large foodstores on market towns and district centres. These combine both retail, economic and traffic impact criteria, thereby addressing the guidance in PPG6 and PPG13. The criteria are summarised in Figure 3.

Figure 3 Predicted Changes – Assessment Criteria

Criteria	Explanation
RETAIL AND ECONOMIC IMPACTS	
Catchment area profile	To what extent will the new store alter the catchment profile of the town. For example, has it increased clawback of expenditure?
Quantitative Impact	Before and after market shares, and trade diversion from the town centre.
Employment Impact	Changes in the level and type of employment.
TRANSPORTATION IMPACTS	
Modal split/Public Transport	Modal split to stores in the area and any likely changes due to the new store
Car ownership/availability	Level of car ownership within the primary catchment area. Whether a car is normally available for the main food shop. This will have an influence on the mode used for food shopping
Car-parking	Provision, pricing and level of use of car-parks in the town and whether there is likely to be any perceptible change as a result of the new store
Linked Trips/Store Location	Are people likely to combine food shopping with other activities on the same trip, particularly within the town centre? Is the occurrence of linked trips likely to be affected by the move to the new store?
Travel distance	Is there likely to be any material change in vehicle mileage as a result of the new store?

(a) Catchment Area Profile and Shopping Patterns

9.20   Any assessment of the changes in shopping patterns following the opening of a new store inevitably relies to a large extent on professional judgements. However, a proper understanding of current shopping patterns enables better informed judgements as to the extent to which shoppers are likely to change their current patterns.

9.21   Our experience of assessing the effects of superstores in market towns and district centres is that the principal area of disagreement between local authorities, and retailers is the extent to which new stores will 'clawback' trade currently lost from the catchment area, and the proportion of the store's trade diverted from the town centre. Our case studies have highlighted that 'clawback/trade diversion' continues to be an area of contention, but provide an insight into the factors which influence this issue.

9.22   Analysts should have a clear appreciation of the relative deficiencies in the current foodstore provision of the centre in question, and the nature of the foodstore provision in competing centres in the catchment area. Similarly, a thorough understanding of the non-food offer in the centre, and how this has changed over the preceding three to five years, will enable more informed assessments to be made about what future changes in shopping patterns can be expected, and what the potential implications of these are likely to be, particularly in regard to the fragility of the centre's retail health.

9.23   Judgements on this key issue can be informed by drawing on the experience to date e.g. consistent and regular health checks, case study evidence, and by a systematic analysis of the likely reasons for outflow, and the realistic prospects for the new store reversing current shopping patterns. Expectations as to the prospect for 'clawback' of trade must be realistic and reflect the centre's position in the retail hierarchy relative to larger centres with overlapping catchments. Where a centre already has a large modern foodstore, the prospects for additional clawback as a result of further stores is likely to be limited (and should be measured as an impact on neighbouring centres).

9.24   The advantage of a modelled approach is that it enables sensitivity analysis of the principal variables. Given the level of judgements inherent in this type of exercise, it may be realistic to confine the analysis to a range of possible changes, based on alternative scenarios. Sensitivity testing should be undertaken to highlight the effects of different judgements about the likely trading pattern of a proposed development.

(b)   Quantitative Impact

9.25   The 'impact' of the proposed development in its simplest form expressed as trade diversion, is calculated by assessing the effect of changed shopping patterns on the turnover of the town centre as a whole at the given design year, which is conventionally one or two years after the store is expected to open. We consider that it is important to provide both an assessment of impact on individual key food retailers and also the convenience sector in the town centre as a whole. This disaggregated analysis allows the implications of different levels of impact and the relative importance of individual key food stores to be taken account of explicitly. In the smallest towns, the principal food supermarket may account for the majority of town centre sales; in such cases the impact on these stores may be a critical consideration.

9.26   The significance of the predicted levels of impact will depend on retailers' resilience, having regard to a range of factors, including current turnover and profitability. Our experience of undertaking the case studies suggests that retailers increasing willingness to divulge information on the turnover/performance of existing stores is likely to be a critical factor in reaching more informed conclusions on this key issue. In the absence of fully reliable census data on sales, other indicators such as evidence of recent investment, level of stock, number of checkouts operating and staffing levels can all provide an indication of the likely performance of foodstores.

9.27   Besides the implications for the closure of key food retailers, having regard to the concerns highlighted in PPG6, the quantum of impact provides an indication of the likely change in the levels of vitality in the centre, as expressed in shopper flows, and associated concerns at the loss of linked trips from other non-food retailers. This is even more difficult to quantify. Our case studies have identified no evidence that out-of-centre stores provide any spin off trade to non-food retailers in neighbouring town centres. Where new stores displace existing more central stores, e.g. Cirencester, they can lead to adverse localised effects in the centre.

9.28   In some market towns and district centres, the effects of a proposed foodstore on the prospects for securing new investment in the centre will be the determining factor. Besides evidence from prospective retailers/investors, analysis of the reduced trading potential of the town provides a good indication of the scope to attract further retail development into the centre needed to secure investor commitment to new development/refurbishment. In the context of smaller market towns and district centres, which we have identified as being particularly vulnerable, any prejudicial effect on the likelihood of securing investment is potentially very serious. These towns are generally already losing market share to larger competing centres, and therefore need to be safeguarded against further erosion of their convenience shopping function.

(c)   Employment Impact

9.29   Our research suggests that there is a widespread deficiency in the availability of accurate retail employment data on a disaggregated town centre/district centre basis. This has been compounded by the inability or unwillingness of food retailers to provide information on the change in employment levels in their stores. As a consequence, we have been unable to draw any substantive conclusions regarding changes in retail employment levels following the opening of large edge/out-of-centre food stores. However, based on national employment levels in the retail sector, there is no evidence of any net increase in employment levels as a consequence of new superstore development.

9.30   We consider that the same types of problems are likely to be encountered when practitioners undertake 'pre-opening' evaluations. Employment levels are an important indicator of economic impact, and further consideration needs to be given as to how problems concerning the availability of data can be resolved. Retailers frequently highlight the jobs to be provided in new stores in support of their proposals. However, without any evidence of the extent to which this represents net additional jobs, only limited weight should be attached to such benefits. We consider there is merit in the argument that a relationship exists between retail and employment impact. In this respect, any displacement of retail employment from the town centre to less central locations would warrant careful consideration.

(d)   Transportation Impacts

9.31   The modelled approach provides a robust basis for assessing the likely changes in shopping patterns, and hence trip lengths. To ensure consistency, this form of analysis should be based on the same predicted changes as the retail and economic impact analysis. This further reinforces the case for a modelled approach to assessing current and future shopping patterns which explicitly identifies anticipated changes in different parts of the proposal's catchment.

9.32   When local authorities, and others, come to use the 'CREATE' method for assessing transportation effects it is suggested the following stages are undertaken:

Stage One	Collection of basic data on, for example, population distribution, bus routes, parking supply, demand, charging, car ownership, etc.
Stage Two	A desktop analysis of how the various criteria set out in this report might be affected if the proposed new store was to take place.
Stage Three	Undertaking relevant interview surveys, if appropriate, to determine factors such as trade draw, existing modal split, existing linkage of trips, etc. This would greatly assist in determining if a new proposed store is likely to have a detrimental or positive effect on travel distance.

9.33   In Stage One, it is important to examine the existing bus services and how they might serve a proposed store. A key question is the proportion of the town's population that will be able to access the store by bus at a reasonable frequency. Given the nature of routes in most market towns a change of bus is likely to be required which could act as a real dis-incentive for bus users. A comparison should be made between services to the new store and those to the town centre.

9.34   Residential walk-in catchment should be determined. However, the assumptions on how far people are prepared or able to walk should not be over-estimated. A maximum distance of 500m is probably reasonable although this specific question has not been addressed as part of this study. Census data should also be examined to determine general levels of car ownership.

9.35   Consideration of parking in the town centre has not proved particularly useful. This is primarily because local authorities do not generally keep accurate records of car park usage. However, in determining the merits of a new store, an important consideration can be the relationship between parking charges at the new store compared with the town centre.

9.36   Based on the above information, a desktop analysis should be undertaken under Stage Two to consider how the criteria set out in Figure 3 might be affected if the new store were built. In particular, key issues should be identified for further investigation under Stage Three.

9.37   The third stage of investigation will usually include a shopper survey to assist in establishing information on existing shopping and travel habits. Careful thought needs to be given to the structure and detail of any interview surveys undertaken. There is a danger in asking too many questions for at least two reasons as follows:-

- the sample answering any particular question can become very small and possibly statistically insignificant;

- People's recollection of circumstances pertaining to a trip only a few weeks ago can be vague and misleading.

9.38   In applying the results of the surveys in order to predict future shopping and travel patterns, a degree of judgement will be required. However, the results of the case studies presented in this report should assist in identifying the more likely effects in the particular circumstances being examined.

9.39   The results of the surveys will be particular helpful in identifying the following:

- Current modal split for food shopping;

- Car availability;

- Location of food shopping and therefore distance travelled; and

- The extent to which trip linkage currently takes place.

9.40   There is significant debate within the profession over whether a detailed quantitative travel distance assessment for new stores should be undertaken. Our experience suggests that such assessments are imprecise due to the complexity of travel patterns. Such patterns are dependent on people's lifestyles and can vary from day to day. In addition, any changes, either positive or negative, are likely to be very small in the context of the overall distance travelled for food shopping. These changes are unlikely to be a determining factor in the decision making process of where to locate a new foodstore; they are likely to be of more relevance in the case of other forms of retail and leisure development.

CHAPTER 10
Policy Implications

Policy Evolution of PPG6

10.1   The original PPG6 entitled 'Major Retail Development' (1988) appeared during a period of unprecedented pressure for major retail development. Whilst it referred to the importance of the vitality and viability of town centres, no checklist of indicators was provided with the guidance, and few local authorities knew how to assess it. The subsequent PPG6 (revised), published in 1993 and entitled 'Town Centres and Retail Development' was indicative of the growing importance that the Government was placing on town centres as shopping environments. The guidance provided a checklist of vitality and viability indicators, and for the first time specifically acknowledged the importance of food retailing in small towns.

10.2   Another significant influence during this period has been the criticism in the House of Commons Environment Select Committee's Fourth Report, *Shopping Centres and Their Future* (October 1994). This focused on the scale of retail development in inappropriate locations, and suggested that future large scale retail development, particularly around market towns, should be accompanied by a comprehensive study of the likely impact. The latest revision to PPG6 published in June 1996 represents an evolution, rather than a radical departure from the earlier version. It places greater emphasis on the primacy of town centres and district centres, and the need to sustain and enhance their vitality and viability.

The Sequential Approach

10.3   The guidance seeks to locate new development, especially retail development, within existing centres. Of particular significance is the sequential test which requires local authorities, in partnership with the private sector, to adopt a positive yet flexible approach to new retail development. Paragraph 1.11 of PPG6 (June 1996) states that:-

'Adopting a sequential approach means that first preference should be for town centre sites, where suitable sites or buildings suitable for conversion are available, followed by edge-of-centre sites, district and local centres and only then out-of-centre sites in locations that are accessible by a choice of means of transport.'

10.4   In this section, we consider in the context of market towns and district centres whether the current sequential approach, particularly in terms of edge-of-centre and out-of-centre locations is appropriate; whether the requirements for impact assessments are sufficiently rigorous; and whether sufficient protection is currently afforded to market towns and district centres.

10.5   The guidance acknowledges that small and historic towns may not have sites which are suitable in terms of size, parking, traffic generation or servicing arrangements for large scale developments in town centres. In terms of food retailing, paragraph 3.13 of PPG6 states that:-

'... the best solution may be an edge-of-centre foodstore with parking facilities, which enables car borne shoppers to walk into the centre for their other business in town, and shoppers who arrive in the centre by other means of transport to walk to the store. One trip can thus serve several purposes, and the new shop is likely to help the economic strength of the existing town centre, be accessible to people without cars, and overall generate less car use. Town centre and edge-of-centre stores facilitate a higher proportion of linked trips.'

Defining Edge-of-Centre

10.6   PPG 6 recognises that the definition of edge-of-centre depends on the specific circumstances of each town, and whilst the limits will be determined by local topography, a guideline of 200m-300m is suggested as a realistic distance for people walking between the store and the town centre. The extent to which edge-of-centre stores in practice contribute to the economic health of town centres has been and continues to be a source of significant debate at public inquiries. In particular, do edge-of-centre locations necessarily facilitate large numbers of linked shopping trips, or do they tend to trade as separate entities to the town centre and draw trade away from it? To assist in clarifying some of the key issues, we undertook two case studies involving edge-of-centre superstores in Cirencester and Warminster.

10.7   The Waitrose superstore is located at the western edge of Cirencester town centre, bounded on its north-west by a principal route into and out of the town centre. The site is approximately 300m from the nearest shops, and just falls within the edge-of-centre designation in PPG6. However, the functional links between the store and the town centre are relatively poor; the principal route between the two is predominantly residential in character with no concentration of shops or services.

10.8   In terms of modal split and propensity for linked trips, our analysis of the edge-of-centre superstore supports the general preference in policy terms for town centre and edge-of-centre development. The edge-of-centre Waitrose secures a materially higher proportion of linked trips than the out-of-centre Tesco. However, of the shoppers currently using the Waitrose, fewer were linking trips with the town centre than before the store opened. This is principally because a large proportion of Waitrose shoppers previously used the town centre Waitrose which subsequently closed when the new store opened.

10.9   Our analysis of Waitrose also suggests that the store has not clawed back significant amounts of trade from competing centres or from the out-of-centre Tesco; the store had not diverted any significant proportion of trade back into Cirencester town centre. Both the household survey and our discussions with the Chamber of Commerce suggests that there is no substantive evidence to show any significant additional spin-off non-food trade being secured as a consequence of the new Waitrose.

10.10   In the Warminster case study, the edge-of-centre Safeway is approximately 300m from the prime retail frontage of the town centre, albeit with its 'back' to the town centre. Whilst the intervening pedestrian route includes crossing a busy traffic light controlled junction and there is a slight incline between the store and town centre, we consider that the route is a relatively 'easy walking distance' in terms of PPG6.

10.11   Again, as was noted in respect to Cirencester, the modal split and propensity for linked trips supports a preference in policy terms for town centre or edge-of-centre development. Nonetheless, whilst the Safeway store is within walking distance of Warminster town centre, some 81% of shoppers visit the store by car, compared with 64% who travel to town centre stores by car. This suggests that Safeway serves a largely car borne catchment, despite the fact it is relatively well integrated with the town centre. An even greater proportion of Waitrose shoppers in Cirencester use a car to visit the edge-of-centre store (94%) suggesting that the availability of a car and convenient car parking are key determining factors as to shoppers' mode of transport rather than the specific location of the store.

10.12   In terms of linked trips our research suggests that edge-of-centre stores do not necessarily generate significantly higher degrees of linkage with town/district centres than out-of-centre stores. Similarly, neither of the new stores in our two edge-of-centre case studies have significantly increased the catchment area of the town, nor have they clawed back large levels of trade from competing centres.

10.13   Whilst both our edge-of-centre case studies exhibited certain features (i.e. an out-of-centre Tesco had already opened in Cirencester, and in both case studies the closure of town centre stores were brought forward), our analysis does suggest that edge-of-centre foodstores may not always be the 'best solution' for small towns; and will not necessarily improve the economic health of existing centres, or generate less car use. Unless strictly controlled there is a danger that edge-of-centre stores can have some of the less desirable characteristics of out-of-centre foodstores, i.e. divert trade from existing centres, but without the potential benefits of significant clawback of expenditure from competing centres.

10.14 We consider that PPG6 should recognise more explicitly that should a need for additional convenience retailing be identified, the best solution for small market towns, and indeed district centres, is for in-centre development, either the development of a new store or the extension of an existing supermarket(s). Only once both of these options have been explored fully should edge-of-centre sites be considered, and even then, only subject to more rigorous scrutiny in respect of their integration with, and impact on, the existing town centre.

10.15 Whilst neither the Waitrose at Cirencester or Safeway at Warminster have materially undermined their respective town centres, they have both been responsible for the transference of relatively large amounts of trade from town centres; principally the result of the closure of Waitrose and Safeway's town centre stores. Our analysis suggests that in order to function, as far as is possible, as part of a town centre, edge-of-centre stores need to be more closely integrated with town centres. In this respect, we consider the current guidelines should be expanded, and require a critical examination of this issue.

10.16 We consider that greater emphasis needs to be placed on the functional linkages between the store and town centre and consideration given to the genuine prospects of linked trips between the two. In the context of market towns, where town centres are generally tightly constrained, in order to achieve a viable link, a site should be very close, if not immediately adjoining the centre. Arguably in larger centres, with a more diverse retail offer, shoppers may be prepared to walk further in order to do a 'linked' shopping trip.

10.17 This suggests that the current edge-of-centre guideline of 200m-300m may be too wide for some small market towns. In addition, we consider that it is important to avoid the artificial elongation of an already extended centre. Based on our experience, we suggest that 800m is a realistic reference point, beyond which a small market town/district centre runs the risk of diluting its retailing focus, and potentially diminishing its character/attractiveness.

Improving Linkages

10.18 In circumstances where there are no town centre opportunities, we consider that in order to make edge-of-centre foodstores function more effectively as part of a town centre, local authorities may need to create the necessary linkages between the two. At present, we consider that in applying the 'edge-of-centre' definition as set out in PPG6, too much emphasis is placed on the physical distance between the store and town/district centre concerned, and insufficient regard to the topography and physical linkages.

10.19 Whilst the appropriateness of a distance criterion will depend on the individual circumstances of each centre, the principal criterion for assessing the extent to which an edge-of-centre food store will complement the town/district centre should always be the 'nature' of the physical links. Promoting linkages to encourage walk-in trade from the store should be seen as priority for local authorities.

10.20 We consider therefore that PPG6 should place greater onus on local authorities and developers to demonstrate clearly that they have undertaken a thorough review of all town centre opportunities before advocating edge-of-centre and out-of-centre locations. This will require a broader ranging assessment of potential town centre sites and a greater commitment on the part of both parties to assessing how existing constraints can be resolved. This may necessitate a greater use of CPO powers; first, to demonstrate the local authority's willingness to use these powers in appropriate circumstances; and second, to highlight their commitment to improving the retail provision of the town centre. In this respect, the increasingly flexible approach being adopted by some foodstore operators to the format, design and scale of their stores is encouraging, and should be supported more strongly by local authorities by strenuous efforts to identify potential town centre sites.

10.21 Where, after thoroughly explaining the availability of town centre opportunities, the only option is an edge or out-of-centre site, our analysis suggests a cautious approach is warranted to considering the possible adverse consequences of development, weighed against the need for new development. If there is no need for further development, local authorities applying the 'sequential test', should resist poorly integrated or inappropriate edge or out-of-centre sites unless they are satisfied that the proposal would sustain and enhance the vitality and viability of the town centre.

10.22 As a postscript to this issue, we consider that where, after careful examination, a site is shown not to meet all the relevant criteria of an edge-of-centre location, it should be treated like any other out-of-centre site. In some cases, preference has been given to the 'next nearest' site. While this may be the most appropriate location, we consider it would be inappropriate to select a compromised or sub-optimal out-of-centre location simply on the basis of its closer proximity to an existing centre, unless some material benefits can be demonstrated.

Out-of-Centre Foodstores

10.23 Where there is a need for new foodstore development, out-of-centre sites should only be considered after fully exploring all potential town centre and edge-of-centre sites, and only then subject to:-

- 'the likely harm to the development plan strategy;

- the likely impact of the development on the vitality and viability of existing centres, including the evening economy, and on the rural economy;

- their accessibility by a choice of means of transport; and

- their likely effect on overall travel patterns and car use.'

10.24 Having regard to our local authority and retailer surveys, and the results of the case studies, we support the rigorous application of the above, and to this end, we consider the CREATE method, discussed in Chapter Nine, provides an effective means of combining both retail and traffic impact assessments.

10.25 The case studies demonstrate a broad range of retail and traffic impacts that can result from out-of-centre foodstores. Some have not in our view undermined the centres in question. However, we consider that there is compelling evidence that out-of-centre stores can in certain circumstances adversely affect the vitality and viability of market towns and district centres. Whilst PPG6 acknowledges the importance of convenience retailing in smaller towns and district centres, we consider a precautionary approach should be taken to all proposals affecting market towns and district centres, which are especially vulnerable to harm from large out-of-centre stores.

Floorspace Threshold for Impact Assessments

10.26 Whilst PPG6 states that retail developments of over 2,500 m^2 gross need to be supported by impact assessments, it also acknowledges that such assessments may occasionally be necessary for smaller developments, such as those likely to have a large impact on market towns or district centres. We consider that these assessments should be required as a matter of course, and should include a clear justification on the part of the applicant for the size of the store proposed having regard to the relative size and nature of the retail provision in the centre or centres likely to be affected. This is particularly relevant in the context of small market towns in relatively rural locations, which hitherto have not accommodated large foodstores, and which could be adversely affected.

10.27 Although it is difficult to be prescriptive in terms of a floorspace threshold, we consider that consistency of approach is needed in order to provide clear guidelines for both local authorities and developers/operators. We suggest that in the context of market towns and district centres, any proposal over 1,000 m^2 of net convenience floorspace (either by way of a new store or an extension to an existing store) in an edge or out-of-centre location should be accompanied by a thorough retail impact assessment.

10.28 In the case of smaller proposals, we consider that the local authority should be able to use its discretion as to whether an impact assessment is strictly necessary, or would assist the authority in determining the proposal. Whilst this is less than any of the foodstores considered in our case studies, we consider that even relatively small stores can potentially have a significant impact on the most vulnerable of smaller market towns and district centres.

10.29 Our case studies suggest that edge-of-centre proposals raise legitimate concerns as to their impact. For the avoidance of doubt, we consider that both edge-of-centre and out-of-centre foodstore proposals should be subject to consistent examination using the CREATE method.

Data Collection

10.30 We support the need for not only a consistency of approach, but also the need for up to date background data. We agree with the retailers contacted in our retailer survey that local authorities should undertake or commission regular household surveys to provide an agreed basis from which parties can assess potential levels of impact. In reality, financial constraints will influence the frequency by which these surveys are carried out, although we would recommend that as a minimum they are undertaken to coincide with the Local Plan review timetable.

10.31 The current guidance places particular emphasis on the role of Local Plans; consideration of retail need is part of the process of determining whether to allocate sites for new retail development. In those circumstances, it is critical that Local Plan retail policies are based on fully up-to-date surveys. While it falls beyond the terms of this study, we would endorse the development of a consistent methodology to determine retail need, in conjunction with the retail industry as the starting point for new foodstore development.

10.32 In terms of accurate floorspace data, we strongly recommend that central government undertake a Census of Distribution. The general paucity of this data at a local level, and the inconsistencies adopted in estimating it serve to undermine the credibility of retail impact assessments. Given the importance of retailing as a

sector, and the emphasis government is placing on planning effectively for town centres, we consider that it needs to make available sufficient funds to carry out an updated Census of Distribution.

10.33 We do not consider that retail impact assessments should as a matter of course be required for town centre proposals. However, there may be circumstances where assessments may be appropriate, for example, where the store proposal represents a significant proportion of overall convenience floorspace in the town centre and/or where the proposal is likely to have a significant effect on other parts of the centre proposal for the town centre as a whole. This approach could be particularly important in historic centres.

Additional Protection for Vulnerable Centres

10.34 Whilst a large number of market towns have already accommodated large edge/out-of-centre foodstores, a number of smaller centres have not. We consider it is these smaller centres which continue to rely to a large extent on their convenience role, and which do not have a strong complementary comparison retail provision or perform a strong tourism function that are potentially the most vulnerable. In our experience, it is not unusual for foodstore operators to target specific regions/areas of the country to maximise not only increasing their profile amongst shoppers, but also securing economic benefits from a reduction in distribution/servicing costs.

10.35 As larger centres are becoming increasingly saturated with large foodstores, and the availability of quality sites is rapidly diminishing, smaller towns not previously targeted by the major foodstore operators are becoming increasingly the focus of their attention. We consider at present PPG6 does not afford sufficient protection to these potentially most vulnerable market towns and district centres. We suggest therefore that any revision to the guidance needs to refer explicitly to these centres where there is particular concern for their continued vitality and viability, and set out clear guidelines as to how proposals in these circumstances will be determined.

10.36 In addition, we would support the further strengthening of advice in the guidance to encourage both local authorities and retailers to take the initiative and to develop a pro-active approach to improving their small market towns and district centres. Whilst Town Centre Management can and does provide an important means to securing widespread improvements to town centres, we consider that in the context of some smaller market towns and district centres, it may not be feasible to set up individual management initiatives.

10.37 In these instances, greater onus should be placed on local authorities to recognise, in the development plan, the particular role of these centres; what needs to be done to improve their attractiveness; and steps which will be taken to secure these improvements.

10.38 The increasing competition afforded by larger towns means that small market towns need to continually improve their offer. In practice, these centres are unlikely to attract large numbers of multiples, and should therefore concentrate on providing more niche/specialist retail and service facilities, as well as improving the quality of their town centre environment. For a number of small market towns, developing and promoting their tourist function will form an integral part of any pro-active town strategy.

CHAPTER 11
Conclusions

Problems of Definition

11.1 'Market town' is a description used in common parlance, but is often used as a generic term to encompass a wide diversity of small historic centres, and not necessarily those that have a general/livestock market. Similarly, there is no universal definition of a district centre; their function varies significantly depending on their size and location relative to dense urban areas.

Challenges Facing Smaller Centres

11.2 The traditional role and function of market towns, in particular, continues to change. Industrial and agricultural development, and shoppers increased mobility and greater expectations have contributed to this process.

11.3 Having concentrated in the 1980s on major cities and towns, foodstore operators seeking to maximise their market share are increasingly focusing on smaller centres. As smaller centres are generally more dependent on convenience retailing to underpin their economic viability, the consequences of this trend are potentially far-reaching.

Research Undertaken to Date

11.4 Whilst research has been undertaken in respect of retail impact methodologies, limited consideration has been given to the specific concerns of market towns and district centres. In terms of transport issues, much has been written on the effects of large foodstores on travel distance, mainly by or sponsored by major foodstore operators.

Local Authority Views

11.5 Almost 45% of local authorities do not consider retail and transport methodologies are adequate. They have expressed concern at the ease with which key variables can be manipulated.

11.6 An alarming number of local authorities (20%) do not require retail impact assessments to be undertaken as a matter of course, and only a small minority (14%) have undertaken post opening surveys to assess the actual impact of large foodstores.

11.7 The lack of a consistent methodology and deficiency in base data (floorspace surveys, information on the turnover/performance of centres) has led to past mistakes in planning control.

Retailer Views

11.8 Leading retailers, including Sainsbury and Tesco, are continuing to develop smaller store formats capable of being accommodated in relatively small centres. This is partly in response to greater restrictions in national planning policy (PPG6), and also a recognition of the benefits of more centrally located foodstores.

11.9 Retailers recognise that large foodstores can have an adverse impact on other foodstores; one retailer referred to impacts of between 3%-40%. Retailers also recognise that impact is not necessarily confined to one store opening, but can relate to several over a number of years (i.e. cumulative impact).

11.10 Although there is some degree of consensus between retailers about the basic methodology for retail and traffic impact assessments, a general concern is the lack of consistent and reliable base data (floorspace, retail turnover and shopping patterns). This concern was a recurring theme throughout the study.

11.11 There appears to be some disagreement between retailers and local authorities as to who should be responsible for providing much of the background data used in retail impact assessments.

Trading Impact

11.12 Our case study research indicates that following the development of large edge/out-of-centre foodstores, main town centre foodstores suffered impacts on their market share of between 13%-50%.

11.13 This wide range of impacts reflects a number of key factors:-

- the relative quality/attractiveness of the new store/operator;

- location of the new store relative to the market town/district centre;

- nature of the catchment area (i.e. whether there is already a dense network of competing foodstores); and

- the relative size of the new foodstore compared with the overall convenience floorspace in the centre itself.

11.14 The decline in market share for the convenience sector as a whole ranged from 21% in St Neots to 64% in Fakenham, and 75% in Warminster.

11.15 Even where an area has a range of out-of-centre and/or edge-of-centre superstores, the addition of a further superstore can have a material impact. The cumulative impact of a succession of new foodstores can undermine the trading potential of town centre foodstores over a number of years.

11.16 Our research shows that impact is not confined solely to other foodstores. In particular, the increasing trend towards incorporating non-food merchandise in large foodstores (e.g. Post Office, pharmacy, dry cleaner and cash points, etc.) means that large foodstores compete with food and non-food facilities in town centres. This is a cause for concern.

11.17 Impact levels suffered by comparison retailers have been less easy to analyse and quantify, particularly distinguishing the effects of large foodstore development from other contributory factors (e.g. economic recession). However, our research suggests that comparison retailers can and have been adversely affected by large foodstore development (e.g. ranging from 3.7%-18.9% in Fakenham). This is potentially most serious in already vulnerable centres.

11.18 The significance of impact will depend on local circumstances. A fall in turnover can have a disproportionately high impact on profitability. Our research shows this can and has led to a lack of investment in improvements/store refurbishments, and in some cases, to store closures (e.g. Fakenham and Leominster).

11.19 In both edge-of-centre case studies (Cirencester and Warminster), the opening of the new stores led to a significant displacement of retail activity from the town centres, largely due to the closure of two town centre foodstores. Whilst neither centre was significantly adversely affected as a whole, neither centre benefitted from the edge-of-centre foodstores.

11.20 Our research shows that market towns and district centres generally have small catchment areas, which can only support a finite number of foodstores. A consequence of the failure to develop a town centre foodstore in favour of allowing out-of-centre or edge-of-centre foodstore to develop is the loss of investment in the town centre. In addition, there is the potential loss of expenditure which a new town centre foodstore may have encouraged.

Employment Impact

11.21 We have been unable to identify accurately any substantive changes in retail employment levels as a consequence of large foodstores. This is because of the lack of accessible, up-to-date and comprehensive employment data at a local level. However, recent research undertaken by the National Retail Planning Forum suggests that there is strong evidence that new superstores have, on average, a negative effect on retail employment.

Impact on Clawback

11.22 Significant claims are made by retailers as to the ability of new superstores to claw back trade, and the benefits derived from this. Our research shows that the extent to which a new out-of-centre and edge-of-centre foodstore will claw back expenditure will vary from centre to centre.

11.23 In our two edge-of-centre case studies, the main effect of the two new stores was to divert trade from the town centre to the edge-of-centre locations, although this result may reflect the particular circumstances of these towns. Our research has shown that where there is already a well established non-central superstore, it is unlikely that an additional edge-of-centre store will achieve the same level of clawback.

11.24 Our case studies have shown that large, highly accessible superstores are likely to achieve higher levels of clawback than smaller, less accessible stores, irrespective of location. For example, in Fakenham some 46% of the trade of the out-of-centre Safeway is derived from clawback of expenditure. However, in this and other case study towns, this has led to no tangible benefit to the town centre.

Impact on Linked Trips

11.25 Not surprisingly, the propensity for linked trips is higher for shoppers using town centre foodstores than edge-of-centre stores. Similarly, edge-of-centre stores generally exhibit greater levels of linkage than out-of-centre foodstores. This appears to support the policy preference for town centre or edge-of-centre stores.

11.26 The change in the propensity of people to link trips after the introduction of a new store varies depending upon the individual circumstances. Whilst some of our case studies show that linked trips increased following the opening of the new non-central foodstore (e.g. Leominster 52% to 63%), there is no evidence of any significant increase in the use of centres for non-food shopping as a result.

Impact on Car Use

11.27 Out-of-centre foodstores generally attract significantly higher levels of car borne trade compared with the town centre store. Where a car is available for food shopping people will almost invariably use it.

11.28 Our research shows that as a result of a new edge-of-centre/out-of-centre foodstore there is a shift in mode towards the private car and away from walk and bus. However, the percentage changes are likely to be relatively small.

11.29 The change in travel distance due to a new store will vary from town to town. In some locations, clawback will lead to a reduction in distance whereas elsewhere there will be little clawback and, potentially, an increase in distance. In both cases the changes are likely to be relatively small in the context of the overall distance travelled for food shopping. It is unlikely that the change in travel distance will be a determining factor in the decision over where to locate a new store.

The Vulnerability of Smaller Centres

11.30 The polarisation of retailing in favour of a smaller number of larger centres means that all market towns and district centres are potentially vulnerable. However, there is evidence that some market towns and district centres are more vulnerable than others.

11.31 Our research suggests that smaller centres which depend on convenience retailing to underpin their economic viability are most at risk. The consequences of impact for 'fragile' centres can be far-reaching; the loss of retailer and investor confidence can cause a spiral of decline which can be difficult to redress.

11.32 In general, larger towns which are not dependent solely on food retailing but have a wider economic base (e.g. a well developed comparison and services function and a clearly defined tourist role) are more resilient to the effects of large foodstores.

Towards a Common Assessment Methodology

11.33 Our research has highlighted the need for a common methodology for assessing impact. We have identified an approach, referred to as a Combined Retail, Economic And Transport Evaluation (CREATE), which we consider provides a comprehensive 'checklist' of criteria necessary to assess the impact of large foodstores. It is not a prescriptive approach, but does provide a consistent basis which should be adopted as a 'best practice guide'. Its use will assist in reducing the amount of 'guesstimation' inherent in retail impact assessments.

Policy Recommendations

11.34 Our study raises key issues for planning policy guidance for market towns and district centres. Greater onus needs to be placed on local authorities and developers to assess more fully town centre opportunities for new foodstore development. This may require the use of CPO powers to demonstrate the local authority's willingness to take the initiative, and to highlight their commitment to improving the retail provision in the town centre.

11.35 Policy guidance should more clearly define need, particularly in respect of particularly vulnerable centres. Where there is no need (i.e. no qualitative or quantitative deficiency), then no additional foodstores should be developed.

11.36 The appropriateness of the 200-300m guideline for edge-of-centre locations set out in PPG6 will vary from centre to centre, although we consider it may be too wide for smaller market towns. Greater emphasis needs to be placed on improving functional linkages between potential edge-of-centre site and town centres. Local authorities need to help improve linkages as it is the links between the store and centre that is the key criterion for assessing the extent to which it will function as part of the centre.

11.37 In addition to comprehensive consideration of the linkages, we consider that a more thorough assessment of the impact of edge-of-centre stores on existing centres is necessary.

11.38 All proposals over 1,000 m² net sales area likely to affect small market towns and district centres should be accompanied by a full Combined, Retail, Economic And Traffic Evaluation (CREATE). This should be undertaken on a consistent basis using common data sources, and should include proper sensitivity testing of key assumptions.

11.39 We consider that in the context of small market towns/district centres, the most informative indicators of a change in vitality and viability are retailer representation, proportion of vacant street property, and the state of the town centre environment. In particular, it is the rate and pattern of change which is important in determining the relative health of these centres.

11.40 The 'time lag' for the effects of large foodstores to manifest themselves can be several years. Vacancy levels are an important indicator of vitality and viability, but changes in turnover and profitability are unlikely to be reflected in increased vacancy levels for several years. The situation is complicated further when centres are affected by the cumulative impact of several new stores over a period of years.

11.41 Providing the appropriate health check indicators are assessed on a regular and consistent basis, we consider that they provide a reasonable basis on which to assess the impact in qualitative terms of large food stores on small market towns and district centres. However, in smaller centres, the impact of a large new store can be significant. In such cases, even relatively healthy centres may be seriously affected.

11.42 Government guidance should provide more emphasis on the responsibility of local authorities and retailers to develop pro-active strategies to improve small market towns. Whilst Town Centre Management initiatives may be appropriate, in the context of smaller centres, we consider that it is primarily the responsibility of local authorities,

through the development plan, to clearly identify a strategy for each town/centre, and set out how this strategy will be put into practice.

11.43 Our research indicates that there is a pressing need for additional data to assist in the consistent application of impact assessments. These include an objective measure of town centre turnover; a reliable database of town centre floorspace; additional research into cumulative impact assessments; and the provision of a clear methodology for assessing on a consistent basis town centre/district centre boundaries.

APPENDIX

CIRENCESTER

Figure 1 **Summary of Assessment Criteria**		
Criteria	**Summary**	**Change**
Catchment area profile	Waitrose draws from a slightly wider catchment area than the town centre Tesco, significantly less than out-of-centre Tesco.	The store has not clawed back significant levels of expenditure from out-of-centre Tesco or from beyond the immediate catchment area. 95% of Waitrose shoppers previously used Cirencester stores.
Shopping Patterns	Proportion of main food shoppers using town centre Tesco decreased slightly, whereas out-of-centre Tesco witnessed a net increase. Out-of-centre Somerfield saw fall in main food shoppers although not transferred to new Waitrose. Generally little change in shopping frequency.	Limited overall change. Almost 80% of current Waitrose main food shoppers previously used the former town centre Waitrose.
Quantitative Impact	Most significant impact resulted from out-of-centre Tesco, although new Waitrose has had a material impact; albeit confined principally to Dyer Street area of town.	- Closure of town centre Waitrose as a result of new Waitrose. Proportion of shoppers undertaking main food shopping in town centre fell from 16% to 8%. - Specialist/independent retailers appear to have been affected most. Full impact may not as yet have been realised.
Employment Impact	Unemployment below average. Higher than average employment in retail sector. No data available to identify changes.	No reliable measures of employment change available.
Modal Split/Public Transport	Greater use of car by those using out-of-centre Tesco compared with town centre. Waitrose falls between the two. One route passed new Waitrose store. None passed out-of-centre Tesco.	Small shift from walk to car mode for shoppers at new Waitrose. No change directly attributable to 2 new superstores.
Linking of Trips	Greater number of combined trips for town centre foodstores and edge-of-centre Waitrose than for out-of-centre Tesco.	
Travel Distance	See comments on frequency of visits and linked trips.	Small increase.
Car Ownership/Availability	Close to national average.	Not measured.
Car Parking	Car parking generally available in town centre. Free parking available at new Waitrose (circa 300 spaces).	Small reduction in turnover of car park closest to former town centre Waitrose. Increased provision serving the town centre.

FAKENHAM

Figure 2 Summary of Assessment Criteria

Criteria	Summary	Change
Catchment area profile	The extent of Fakenham's catchment area has widened by an additional postcode sector after the opening of Safeway. In contrast the town centre's catchment area has narrowed in extent.	Safeway has increased the total in and out of centre market share to 54% from 41%. However, this has been at the expense of the town centre's market share falling to a third of its previous level (5%).
Shopping Patterns	Fakenham town centre's comparison shopping catchment area covers the whole of the survey area and thus is now larger than the equivalent town centre convenience shopping catchment. Approximately a third of Safeway's shoppers previously used the out of centre Rainbow with 17% from the town centre. However, given the small scale of town centre convenience shopping, this is a significant effect.	The town centre has also lost much of its periodic bulk convenience shopping function, with top-up shopping accounting for a higher proportion of shoppers. Outflow of expenditure to Kings Lynn has been reduced. Fakenham town centre's market share has decreased substantially in all sectors around the town.
Quantitative Impact	There has been a spin-off effect with comparison shops experiencing falling turnovers, although declining trading conditions were occurring in the run up to the opening of the store.	The ex-Lo-Cost store shut after briefly reopening as Spar. The proportion of people undertaking their main food shopping in the town centre has fallen by 64% with a 50% impact on the main foodstore of Budgens.
Employment Impact	Changes in employment are related to business closures/openings rather than any changes to the number of people employed per shop.	Employment levels in comparison retailers have increased due to the expansion of W J Aldiss. There have also been employment losses due to the high number of business closures, partially been mitigated by new openings.
Modal Split/Public Transport	99% of trips to Safeway are carried out by car. There is greater walk-in trade in the town centre.	Overall modal split for customers visiting all stores has not changed. Therefore, there has been a transference of car borne trade from the town centre to out of centre.
Linked Trips/Store Location	New Safeway is mainly a one-stop shopping destination.	Significant effect on town centre due to linkages with other town centre uses by shoppers previously using Lo-Cost, Budgens and other stores.
Travel Distance	Slight reduction in distance travelled due to limited transfer of trade from King's Lynn. Likely to be offset by change in modal shift, increase in frequency of visits and reduction in linked trips.	Net effect is broadly neutral.
Car Ownership/Availability	Above national average.	Virtually no change.
Car Parking	Spare capacity exists in the car parks except on market days.	No information is available on changes in car park usage.

ST NEOTS

Figure 3 Summary of Assessment Criteria

Criteria	Summary	Change
Catchment area profile	The extent of St Neots' catchment area has not changed since the opening of Tesco	Tesco has increased the total in and out-of-centre market share of St Neots by 15% points, with the town centre market share falling from 24% to 18%.
Shopping Patterns	St Neots town centre comparison shopping catchment area is slightly smaller than its pre-Tesco convenience catchment. However, non-food trade retention was higher. Approximately a third of Tesco's shoppers previously used shops in St Neots town centre with 22% from Waitrose.	There has been a slight increase in the frequency of main food shopping trips. There has not been a significant change in the proportion of main food expenditure spent in the town centre stores. Outflow of expenditure to Bedford and Huntingdon has been reduced substantially. St Neots market share in all sectors around the town has increased significantly for food shopping.
Quantitative Impact	Main impact has fallen on Waitrose (38% fall in market share). Virtually no effect on non-food retailers. The impact in market share on Somerfield has been considerably smaller (13%).	No town centre closures of convenience retailers. Proportion of shoppers undertaking main food shopping in the town centre has fallen from 24% to 17%.
Employment Impact	Unemployment in the St Neots area has been consistently below the national average and is falling. Changes appear to be confined to the convenience shopping sector.	One of the main convenience retailers cut its employment levels after experiencing a fall in turnover. Employment levels have now risen again as a result of Sunday trading. No apparent effect on employment in non-food retailers.
Modal Split/Public Transport	Overall modal split of customers visiting all stores has not changed significantly. Approximately 20% of shoppers to Waitrose and Somerfield are walk-in trade. Tesco is almost completely reliant on the car.	There has been a noticeable shift away from bus travel from shoppers now choosing to use Tesco.
Linked Trips/Store Location	New Tesco is mainly a one-stop shopping destination with very little linkage to St Neots town centre.	Little effect on town centre as shoppers who transferred from Waitrose and Somerfield were mainly one-stop shoppers.
Travel Distance	There has been a reduction in travel distances from people no longer choosing to shop in Bedford, but at the same time an increase in distances for those living to the north of St Neots and now using Tesco together with the reduction in linked trips.	Net effect on travel distance is broadly neutral.
Car Ownership/Availability	Above national average.	Virtually no change.
Car Parking	No evidence available on change in car park usage.	

WARMINSTER

Figure 4 Summary of Assessment Criteria

Criteria	Summary	Change
Catchment area profile	The new Safeway store draws trade from a slightly smaller catchment area but achieves a larger market share than the former Three Horseshoes Safeway store.	The new Safeway store achieves a higher market share in a number of postcode sectors compared with the former Three Horseshoes store. Considering the new Safeway store as part of the town, its overall market share has increased by 20%.
Shopping Patterns	Respondents previously using the Three Horseshoes Safeway store have largely transferred to the new Safeway. A small proportion of respondents previously using the Normans store in Cockerton have transferred to Safeway. There has been an increase in the frequency of visits to the town centre for main food shopping.	In excess of 80% of respondents using the Three Horseshoes store have transferred to the new Safeway. The new Safeway has resulted in a 12% increase in respondents undertaking a main food shop in the town centre more frequently than 2-3 times a week.
Quantitative Impact	The new store has drawn the majority of its trade from the Three Horseshoes Mall. The Gateway store has closed the Normans at Cockerton have suffered substantial impact, although the level of impact are disproportionately high due to the small initial market share of the store.	The Safeway/Lo-Cost in the Three Horseshoes Mall suffered an 86% impact. The Normans at Cockerton suffered a 50% impact. The Gateway store has closed (100% impact). Other town centre food retailers have also suffered 100% impact.
Employment Impact	Unemployment below national average. Higher than average representation in manufacturing sectors. The introduction of two large new foodstores (Safeway and Lidl) suggests an overall increase in the levels of retail employment.	No reliable measures of employment change available.
Modal Split/Public Transport	The majority of respondents using the Safeway store travelled by car. Respondents using town centre stores (excluding the new Safeway) for main food shop use their car less and a significant proportion walked to the centre. The Safeway store has a bus stop outside the store entrance.	77% of Safeway respondents travelled by car. In contrast, 54% of main food respondents in the town centre used cars and 30% walked to the centre. Overall, the new store has not resulted in a change in modal choice.
Linking of Trips	Those respondents making linked trips to the town undertook a similar range of activities to those previously undertaken by respondents using the Three Horseshoes store.	Overall, little effect.
Travel Distance	Data does not indicate a discernible change.	N/A
Car Ownership/Availability	Overall, there has been a reduction in the use of the car for main food shopping based on trade drawn from Trowbridge.	Car usage for main food shop by Safeway respondents has decreased by 3% while car availability has increased by 2%.
Car Parking	Free surface level car parking available in Warminster.	No significant change.

NORTHFIELD

Figure 5 Summary of Assessment Criteria

Criteria	Summary	Change
Catchment area profile	The Safeway store has increased market share drawing from all 16 postcode sectors in the catchment area. Significant trade has been drawn from postcode sectors that were previously attributable to Rubery stores.	The store has not clawed back a significant amount of trade from existing stores in the catchment area
Shopping Patterns	There has been a slight increase in the frequency of visits to Northfield stores. The frequency of visit to Rubery stores has remained constant. A number of Safeway shoppers continue to use a number of other foodstores in Northfield, Rubery and Selly Oak.	Visits 2-3 times a week to Sainsbury's, Northfield has increased by 11%. Visits to other Northfield stores 2-3 times a week has also increased by 12%. Birmingham city centre remains the main centre for non-food shopping.
Quantitative Impact	The Safeway store has had sizeable impacts on the Tesco store in Northfield and foodstores in Rubery.	No main foodstores in the catchment area have closed. Although a number of independent retailers in Rubery have closed after the store opening. The Safeway store had a 33% impact on the Tesco, Northfield and a 25% impact on foodstores in Rubery. The market share for the Sainsbury's, Northfield has remained static while the market share for the Sainsbury's at Selly Oak has actually increased by 18%.
Employment Impact	Birmingham is over-represented in manufacturing sectors with a disproportionate amount of unemployment in this sector compared with service sectors. The opening of a new store without significant closures elsewhere suggests an overall increase in employment.	No reliable measures of employment change available.
Modal Split/Public Transport	A significant number of Safeway shoppers visit the store by car. In contrast, the shoppers in Northfield and Rubery exhibit a more diverse range of modal split. The new Safeway store has a bus stop outside the store entrance.	86% of Safeway respondents visited the store by car. Only 40% of respondents using Sainsbury's, Northfield used their car. 36% travelled by bus to the store.
Linking of Trips	A significant proportion of the trips to the Safeway store are for a single purpose. Those linked trips undertaken by Safeway shoppers include a more limited range than that undertaken by Northfield and Rubery shoppers.	Decline in number of linked trips (43% to 25%).
Travel Distance	Increased use of the car and the limited number of linked trips suggests an increase in travel distances.	No reliable measures in changes of travel distance.
Car Ownership/Availability	Below the national average.	No changes actually attributable to the new store.
Car Parking	Both Northfield and Rubery are well served by surface level car parking.	No change directly attributable to the new store.

LEOMINSTER

Figure 6 Assessment Criteria for Leominster

Criteria	Summary	Change
Catchment area profile	Leominster's total catchment area has widened since the opening of Safeway. In contrast, the catchment area of the town centre has narrowed in extent.	Safeway has increased the total in and out-of-centre market share of Leominster by 12 percentage points, whilst the town centre market share has fallen by 10 percentage points.
Shopping Patterns	Approximately 45% of Safeway shoppers previously used shops in Leominster town centre with 24% previously shopping at Somerfield.	Leominster town centre's convenience market share has decreased in all sectors around the town.
	The Catchment area of food retailers in Leominster town centre is now smaller than the equivalent catchment area for comparison shopping. Similarly, penetration rates are generally below those of the comparison goods sector.	Outflow of expenditure to competing centres (in particular, Hereford) has been reduced.
		Slight increase in the frequency of main food shopping trips in Leominster town centre. No significant change in the proportion of main food expenditure in Somerfield, but marked decrease in 'other Leominster' town centre foodstores.
Quantitative Impact	Significant impact on market share of town centre food retailers of approximately 43% (including a 33% impact on Somerfield).	Two centrally located town centre supermarkets have closed (Saverite and Lo-Cost), one of which remains vacant. Kwik Save have opened an edge-of-centre store (November 1994).
	Anecdotal evidence to suggest some decline in turnover of comparison retailers. Although other factors involved.	
		Proportion of shoppers undertaking main food shopping in the town centre has fallen from 23% to 13%.
Employment Impact	Unemployment in Leominster continues to be below the national average.	Decline in the number of convenience retailers and modest fall in number of comparison retailers. Estimates suggest a loss of some 47 jobs in the town centre as a result of shop closures.
Modal Split/Public Transport	Approximately 20% of shoppers using Somerfield in Leominster town centre walk. In contrast, the majority (96%) of shoppers using Safeway travel by car.	Overall modal split for customers visiting all stores has not changed.
		For Safeway customers, there has been a modal shift towards travel by car and a decline in proportion of shoppers walking to the store and the use of the bus.
Linked Trips/Store Location	Fewer linked trips are undertaken between the Safeway and Leominster compared to town centre foodstores in Leominster. Nonetheless degree of linkage is relatively high.	Evidence of slight increase in propensity of Safeway customers to undertake linked trips with Leominster town centre.
Travel Distance	Slight reduction in distance travelled due to limited transfer of trade from Hereford. Although large proportion of Safeway shoppers live outside Leominster and immediate area.	Net effect on travel distance is broadly neutral.
Car Ownership/Availability	Above national average	No evidence of significant change.
Car Parking	No evidence available on change in car parking	

FERNDOWN

Figure 7 Summary of Assessment Criteria of Ferndown

Criteria	Summary	Change
Catchment area profile	Prior to Sainsbury's opening, Ferndown District Centre's main food catchment extended to all postcode sectors within the survey area. Post opening, the District Centre's catchment has narrowed and no longer includes two postcode sectors.	Sainsbury has increased the total in and out-of-centre market share from 30% to 39%. The town centre's market share has fallen from 30% to 21%.
Shopping Patterns	Approximately 37% of Sainsbury shoppers previously used Tesco in Ferndown District Centre, 9% used Safeway, and only 4% used other Ferndown foodstores.	Ferndown District Centre's market share has decreased, principally as a result of Safeway's closure.
	Ferndown District Centre's comparison shopping catchment is very discrete, and significantly smaller than its convenience shopping catchment. This reflects the limited comparison goods offer in contrast to the relatively strong convenience goods offer (Tesco).	The District Centre has retained its periodic bulk convenience shopping function (Tesco), with top-up shopping being provided for by the smaller food retailers.
		Outflow of expenditure to Poole and Ringwood has been reduced.
Quantitative Impact	There has been no obvious fall in turnover of comparison retailers as a result of Sainsbury. However general economic conditions have had a downward effect on turnover levels.	Safeway have closed and their unit still remains vacant. Kwik Save are also due to close imminently. No substantive evidence to suggest either is directly attributable to Sainsbury, although likely to have been a factor.
		The proportion of people undertaking their main food shopping in the District Centre has fallen by 30% with a 13% impact on the market share of the main foodstore of Tesco.
Employment Impact	No up to date information on employment change by sector is available.	The closure of Safeway and imminent closure of Kwik Save are likely to have had a negative effect on employment levels, although this may have been more than offset by jobs created at Sainsbury (206 full-time equivalent).
Modal Split/Public Transport	95% of trips to Sainsbury are carried out by car. There is greater walk-in trade in the district centre (12% walk to Tesco). The use of public transport (bus) is very low.	Sainsbury has had virtually no effect on modal choice of customers of Sainsbury's or customers of other stores in the survey area.
Linked Trips/Store Location	Sainsbury is mainly a one-stop shopping destination, although there is reasonable level of linkage with the district centre.	There has been no significant change in the propensity of Sainsbury's customers to link trips with Ferndown District Centre.
Travel Distance	Likely to be a slight reduction in distance travelled due to limited transfer of trade from Poole and Ringwood. However, 40% of Sainsbury's customers live outside the Ferndown area, and may therefore have to travel further than prior to Sainsbury's opening.	Net effect is broadly neutral.
Car Ownership/Availability	Above national average.	Virtually no change.
Car Parking	Car parking is generally adequate with no obvious signs of congestion.	There is no survey data to suggest a discernible change in parking patterns or usage.

ASHBY-DE-LA-ZOUCH

Figure 8 Assessment Criteria

Criteria	Summary	Change
Catchment area profile	Ashby's catchment area has been extended over more postcode sectors and the town's overall market share has increased.	The Tesco store has increased Ashby's overall market share from 8% to 15%.
Shopping Patterns	The overall market share (including town centre and out-of-centre stores) for Coalville, Swadlincote and Ashby has increased.	The market share for Coalville has increased from 28% to 30%, for Swadlincote from 19% to 22% and Ashby from 8% to 15%.
	The Somerfield store is now visited more frequently and appears to perform a top-up shopping function.	Respondents visiting Somerfield, Ashby 2-3 times a week has increased from 39% to 51%.
	The modern food superstores (Tesco and Sainsbury's) perform a bulk shopping function.	The majority of respondents using these stores (80%) purchase in excess of 50% of their main food shopping.
Quantitative Impact	The household survey has not recorded a significant impact on other stores as a result of the Tesco opening.	The Kwik Save sore, Ashby, has recorded a 33% impact. The Somerfield store, Ashby, has not recorded a change in market share. However, the store manager reports a 20%-25% impact.
	The Tesco store has drawn the majority of its trade from respondents who previously used the Somerfield store in Ashby.	32% of Tesco respondents previously shopped at Somerfield in Ashby.
Employment Impact	There have been no major store closures since the Tesco opening.	There is no evidence to suggest a change in levels of employment.
Modal Split/Public Transport	The modal split for main food shoppers has changed little after the Tesco opening. Town centre food shoppers (Somerfield stores in Ashby and Swadlincote) have a more diverse modal split.	Respondents using modern out-of-centre food superstores (Morrisons, Sainsbury's and Tesco) predominantly travel by car (in excess of 85%). Only 50% of Somerfield respondents travel by car, and in excess of 15% walk to the stores in Ashby and Swadlincote.
Linked Trips/Store Location	Town centre stores have a higher proportion of linked trips than out-of-centre stores.	Slight increase in linked trips (46% to 54%).
Travel Distance	The Tesco store has clawed back respondents who previously conducted their shopping outside Ashby's immediate catchment area.	The Tesco has resulted in an overall decrease in distance travelled.
Car Ownership/Availability	In excess of the national average.	No overall change
Car Parking	Shortage of short term spaces in Ashby.	No evidence

PORTCHESTER

Figure 9 Assessment Criteria

Criteria	Summary	Change
Catchment area profile	The new Tesco store has increased Portchester's overall market share and draws expenditure from 13 of the 14 postcode sectors.	The Tesco store achieves a 12% market share in the catchment area, and the market share of the Somerfield, West Street has increased by 1% from 3% to 4%.
Shopping Patterns	The Tesco store has drawn the majority of its trade from the modern food superstores in Fareham, Cosham and stores in Portsmouth city centre.	The Tesco store has drawn 14% of its respondents from both the Sainsbury's and Asda stores in Fareham, 16% from Sainsbury's, Fitzherbert Road, Cosham and 19% from Portsmouth stores.
	The frequency of visit to Fareham town centre stores has increased after the Tesco opening. The frequency of visit to modern superstores in Fareham (Asda and Sainsbury's) has stayed the same but has increased for the Sainsbury's in Cosham.	The frequency of visit 2-3 times a week to 'other Fareham stores' has increased from 29% to 51%. The frequency of visit to Sainsbury's at Cosham 2-3 times a week, has increased from 27% to 38%.
	Despite the increase in frequency of visit to the Sainsbury's at Cosham, this and the other modern food superstores (Tesco at Portchester and Sainsbury's at Fareham) still satisfy a bulk food shopping role.	The three modern food superstores (Sainsbury's at Fareham and Cosham and Tesco at Portchester) have the majority of respondents (over 80%) spending in excess of 50% of their main food shop in the store.
Quantitative Impact	The market share of Portchester main foodstore, Somerfield, has actually increased since the Tesco store opened. Conversely, the store manager reports a 2%-3% impact on turnover.	The Somerfield's market share has increased from 3% to 4%. The relatively short period, less than 18 months, since the Tesco opening may mean shopping patterns have not settled down in order for the household survey to properly predict the store's impact.
	The market share for Sainsbury's stores in Fareham and Cosham and the Asda store in Portland Road, Waterlooville have also increased.	The market share for Sainsbury's in Fareham and Cosham have increased from 12% to 15% and 9% to 10% respectively. The Asda store, Waterlooville, has increased its market share from 14% to 16%. The trend for modern stores of the big four food retailers (Tesco, Sainsbury's, Safeway and Asda) to extend their market shares is a national phenomena.
Employment Impact	There have been no major store closures as a result of the Tesco opening and therefore no apparent reduction in retail employment.	No evidence to suggest a significant change.

PORTCHESTER (CONTINUED)

Figure 9 Assessment Criteria

Criteria	Summary	Change
Modal Split/Public Transport	The majority of Tesco respondents visit the store by car.	85% of Tesco respondents visit the store by car.
	Since the store opening, more respondents use their car for main food shopping.	Car borne travel has increased from 78% to 85%.
Linked Trips/Store Location	Respondents using the Tesco store exhibit a higher propensity to undertake linked trips when compared to other case study stores.	65% of Tesco respondents undertake a linked trip, this compares with 63% of Safeway respondents in Leominster.
	The new store has not materially affected respondents propensity to make linked trips.	Respondents undertaking linked trips before Tesco opened (67%) compared with 65% now.
Travel Distance	There has been a slight reduction in distance travelled for main food shopping, however, this has been offset by an increase in frequency of main food shopping.	No overall change.
Car Ownership/Availability	The level of car availability has not changed materially in the catchment area.	Approximately 80% of respondents had access to a car before and after the store opening.
Car Parking	There have been no before or after car park utilisation surveys.	No evidence.

BIBLIOGRAPHY

BDP Planning and the Oxford Institute of Retail Management (1994) *The Effects of Major Out-of-Town Retail Developments.* London HMSO

Boots The Chemist and the Civic Trust Regeneration Unit (1994) *Caring For Our Towns and Cities.* Boots The Chemist

Boots The Chemist (1998) *The Impact of Out-of-Centre Food Superstores on Local Retail Employment.* The National Retail Planning Forum

Department of the Environment (1994) *Vital and Viable Town Centres: Meeting the Challenge.* London HMSO

Department of the Environment (1994) *PPG13: Transport.* London HMSO

Department of the Environment (1994) *Shopping Centres and their Future. The Fourth Report from the House of Commons Select Committee on the Environment.* London HMSO

Department of the Environment (1995) *Shopping Centres and their Future. The Government's response to the Fourth Report from the House of Commons Select Committee on the Environment.* London HMSO

Department of the Environment (1996) *PPG6: Town Centres and Retail Developments.* London HMSO

Department of the Environment (1997) *Report on Shopping Centres by the House of Commons Select Committee on the Environment.* London HMSO

Department of the Environment, Transport and the Regions (1997) *The Government's response to the Fourth Report from the House of Commons Select Committee on the Environment.* London HMSO

Derbyshire County Council (1983) *Two of a Kind?* Derbyshire CC

Donaldsons, Healey & Baker and Association for Town Centre Management (1994). *Effectiveness of Town Centre Management*

Drivers Jonas (1992) *Retail Impact Assessment Methodologies.* Scottish Office

Institution of Highways and Transportation (1994) *Guidelines for Traffic Impact Assessment*

JMP Consultants (1991) *Seasonal and Daily Variation in Travel to Retail Stores*

Parker A (1995) *Market Towns and Foodstores: A New Policy Approach.* Estates Gazette January 21 1995

Rapleys for Safeway (1997) *The Effects of New Foodstores in Six Market Towns*

RPS Nigel Moor for Tesco (1994) *PPG13 Applied to Retail Development: The Minimisation of Carbon Dioxide and other Polluting Emissions*

Rural Development Commission (1996) *Promoting Jobs and Communities in Rural England.* Rural Development Commission

Somerfield/Gateway (1994) *Backing Britain's High Streets – A Memorandum of Evidence to the House of Commons Select Committee on the Environment.* Gateway Foodmarkets

Telephone Surveys Ltd for J Sainsbury (1993) *Food Shopping and the Car.*

Transport Studies Unit, University of Oxford for J Sainsbury (1993) *Superstore Impact on Travel Patterns*

TRICS for Safeway (1995) *Traffic and Parking at Food Retailing*

TRICS Conference Papers (1995)

UK Government (1990) *This Common Inheritance.* London HMSO

Verdict (1997) *Out of Town vs High Street.* Verdict Research Ltd

Verdict (1998) *Grocers and Supermarkets.* Verdict Research Ltd

Williams H (1995) The Future of Country Towns Conference hosted by the Town & Country Planning Association (Scotland) in Perth – *Country Towns: Retail Saturation?* J Sainsbury

Printed in the United Kingdom for the Stationery Office
J65139   C10   11/98   65536   45/44879